HOLLYWOOD BROADWALK

Floridian Paradise

Hollywood Broadwalk

Floridian Paradise

■ ■ ■

photographs

by NADIA RUSS

NeoPopRealismPRESS

First time published in 2013 by NeoPopRealism PRESS

PO BOX 366
New York, NY 10013
NeoPopRealismPRESS@mail.com

Hollywood Broadwalk: Floridian Paradise
by NeoPopRealism PRESS and Nadia Russ

Front cover image: *Pierce Street & Broadwalk* by Nadia Russ.
Back cover image: *Living near Broadwalk at Arizona street, in a house where the movies have been made* by Nadia Russ.

ISBN-13: 978-0615937663
ISBN-10: 0615937667

13 14 15 16 17 10 9 8 7 6 5 4 3 2 1

Published in the United States of America
Language: English

This book offers a collection of 48 photographs taken by Nadia Russ in Hollywood, Florida in 2013.

www.neopoprealism.org

CONTENT

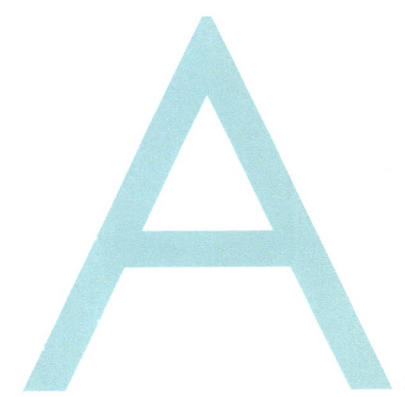NTRODUCTION

An idea about making a photography book "Hollywood Broadwalk: Floridian Paradise" came in my mind immediately after I saw Hollywood beach. Same evening after my arriving to Hollywood, two men who were on a mission to expand their church by inviting there new people, started a conversation with me, asking a question: "What is Paradise?" It was on Broadwalk, and I said: "It is Hollywood beach." It was my first impression about this unique place - beautiful, warm, and peaceful.

Hollywood beach is not super fashionable, it has past century's charm. This part of the Atlantic Ocean's shore - Hollywood Broadwalk - is not like any other broadwalk. It fascinates with its low energy beauty. There, everything is small, not pretentious, simple and attractive by special Hollywood's charm: restaurants and cafes, stores and hotels, benches on sidewalk and bicycles' lane, Hollywood Beach Theater. There's a children's water playground at Charnow Park, and other attractions. For many years it is the international tourists' center. Many Canadians have made it their second home.

The Hollywood Beach Broadwalk stretches nearly 2.5 miles along the Atlantic Ocean and by *Travel + Leisure* magazine is named one of America's Best Beach Boardwalks. It hosts pedestrians, bicyclists, rollerbladers, joggers, and others.

Today, the technological and cultural progress changes everything. In 2013, the global constructions came to Hollywood Beach with such project like Margaritaville resort. It suppose to change the whole City of Hollywood and particularly the Broadwalk. However, I hope that the Hollywood Beach Broadwalk will not lose its charm and beauty, which attract and stimulate aesthetic senses and romantic feelings. Photographs featured in this book have been taken on the Hollywood Broadwalk in 2013.

Nadia Russ

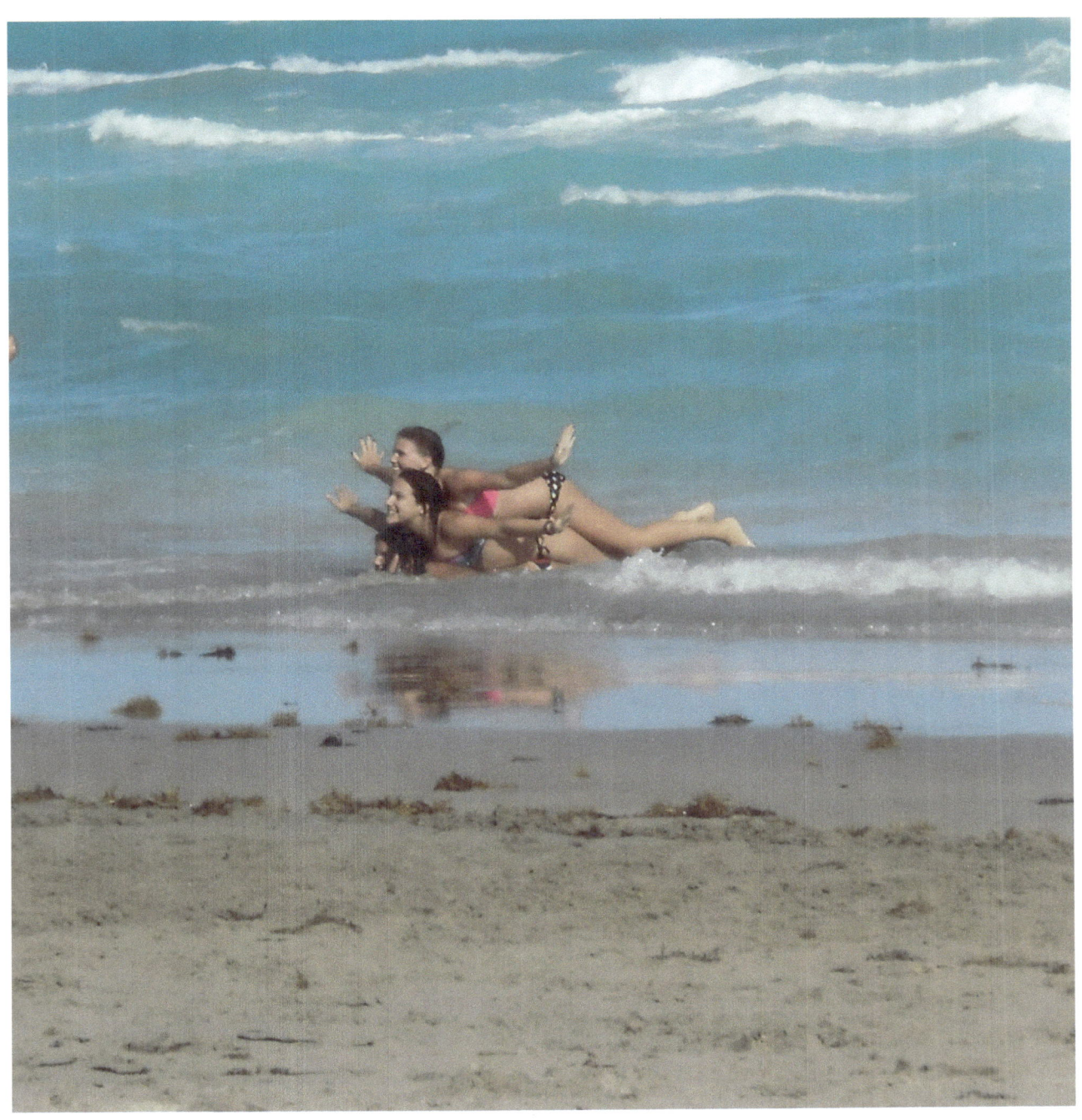

Fun under sun.

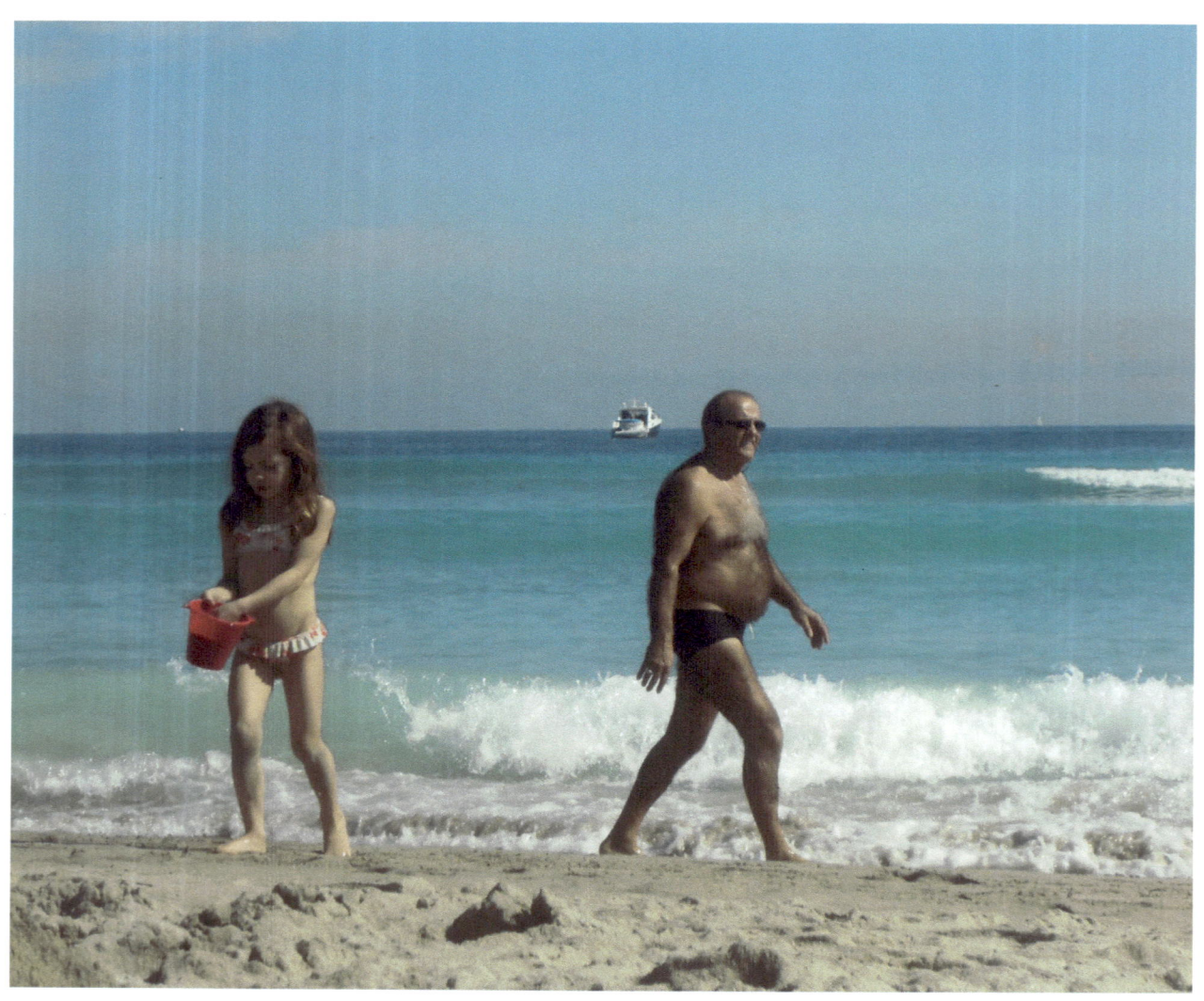

Beach activities

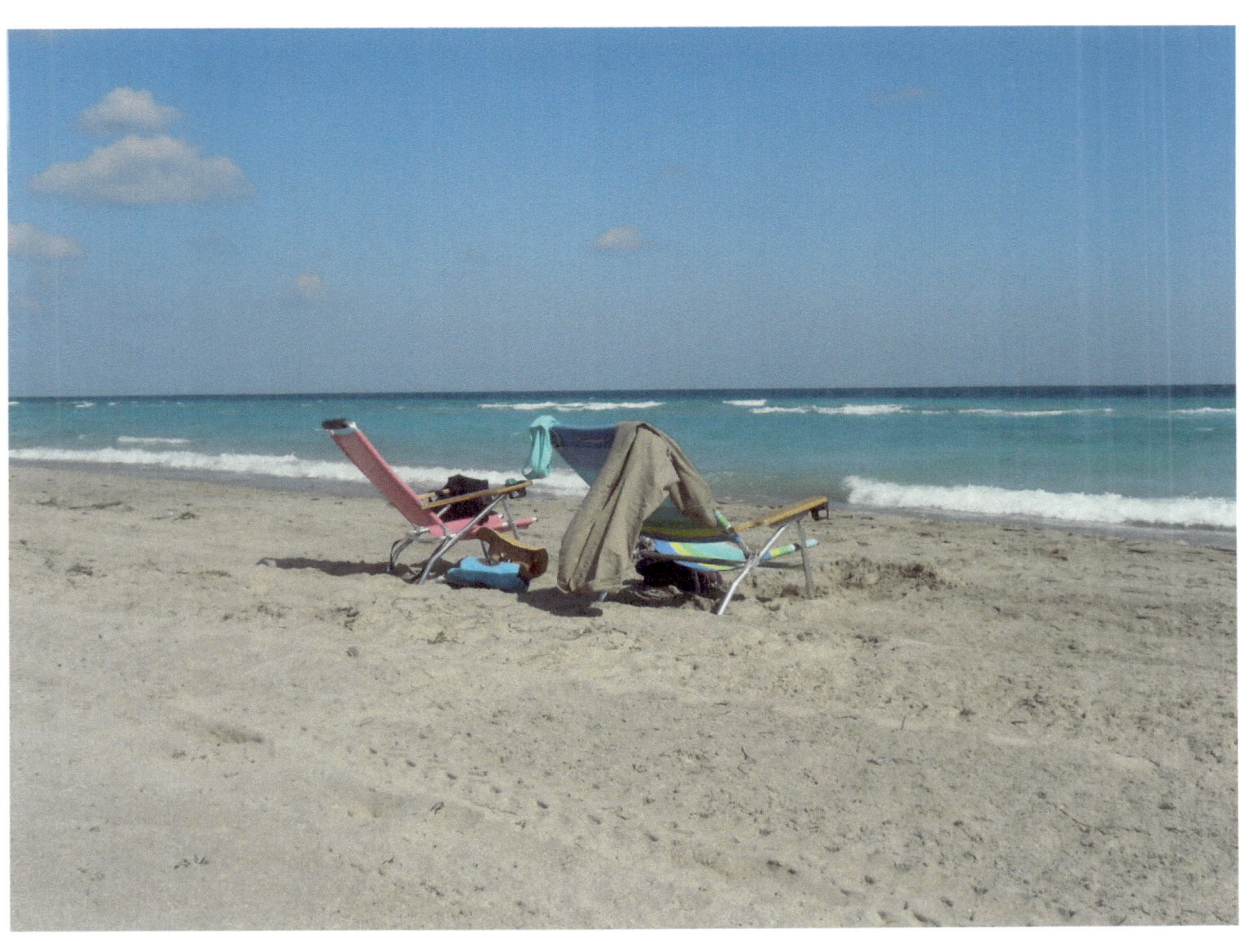

Lost in the sea.

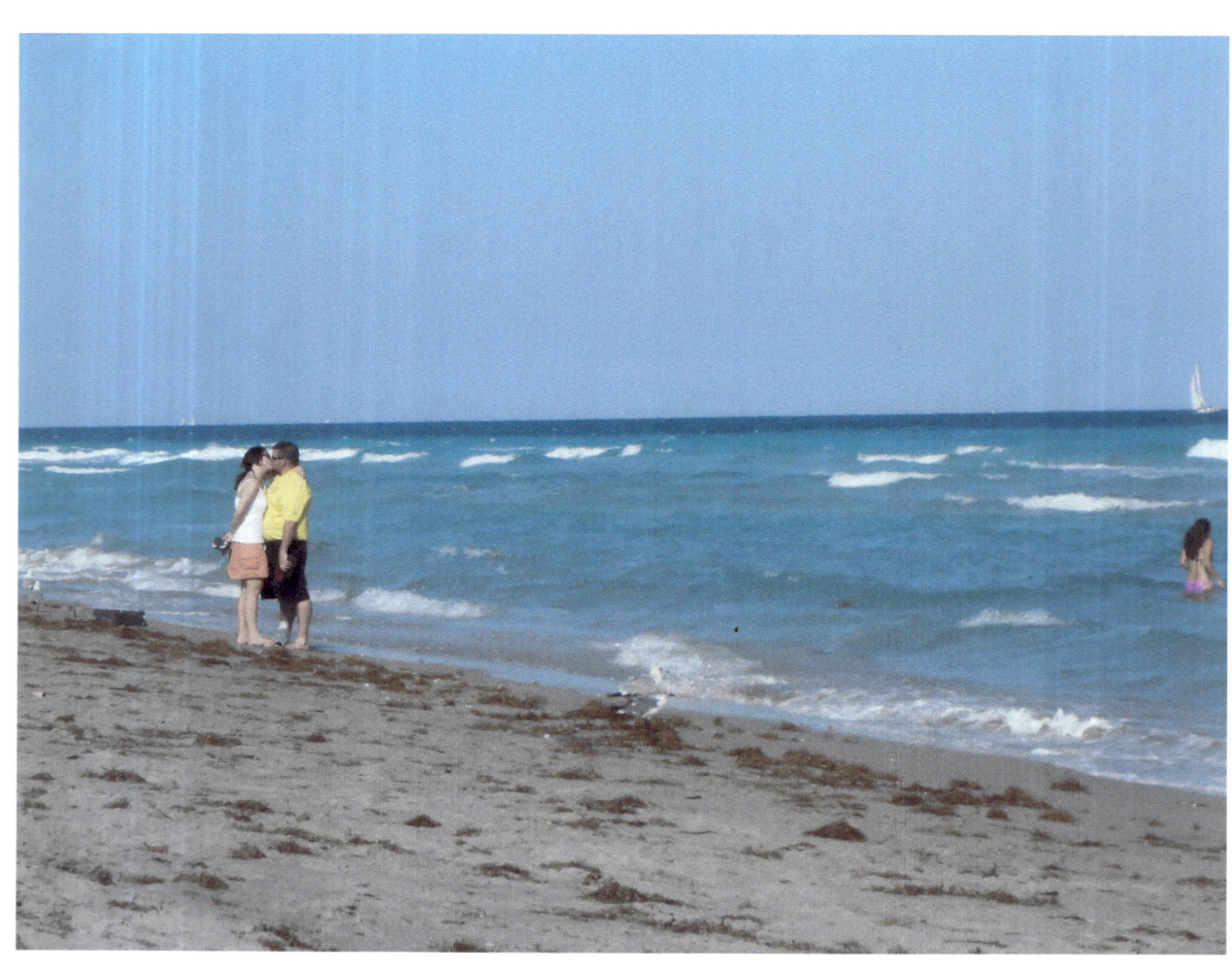

A kiss.

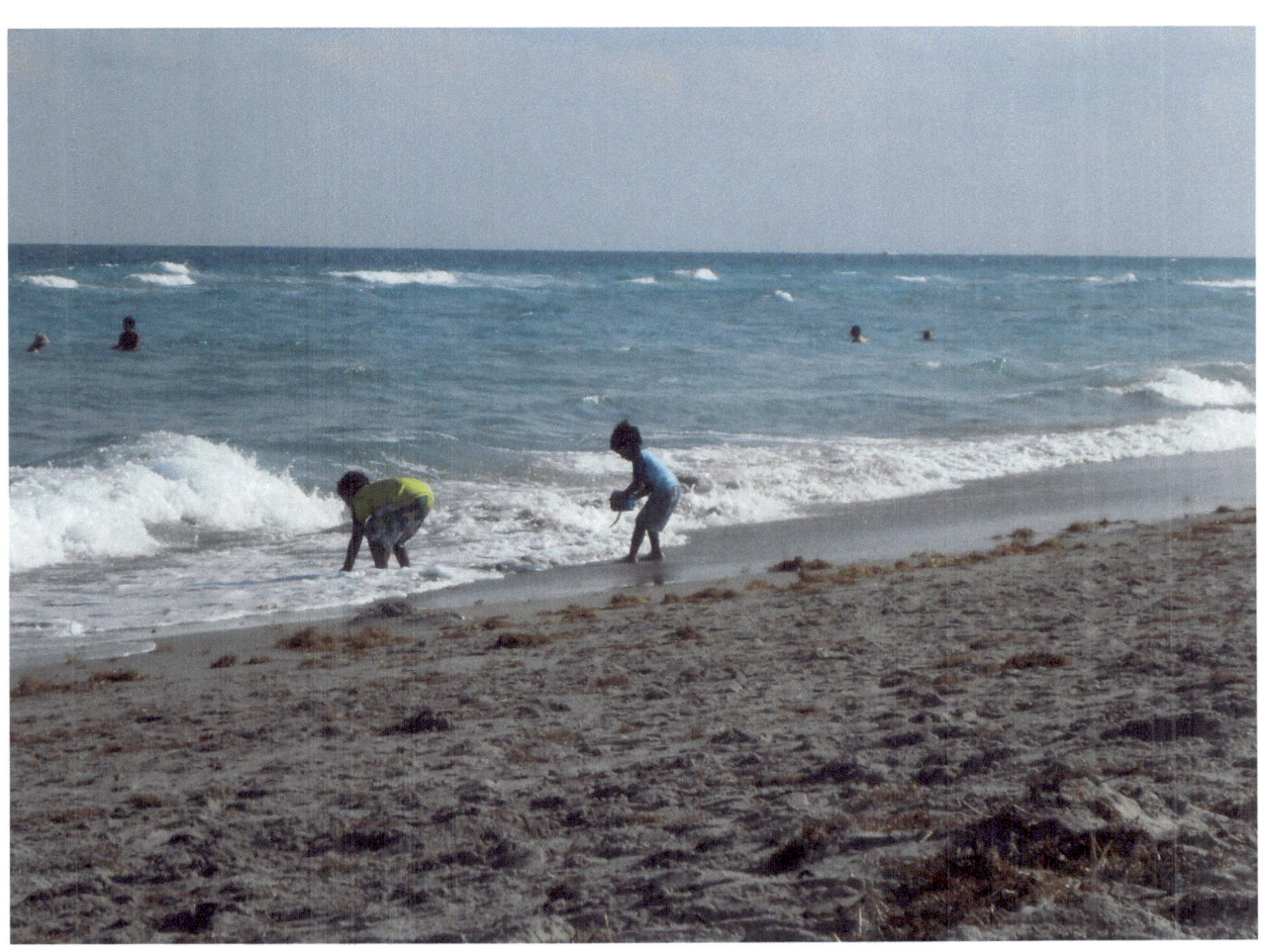

Busy time.

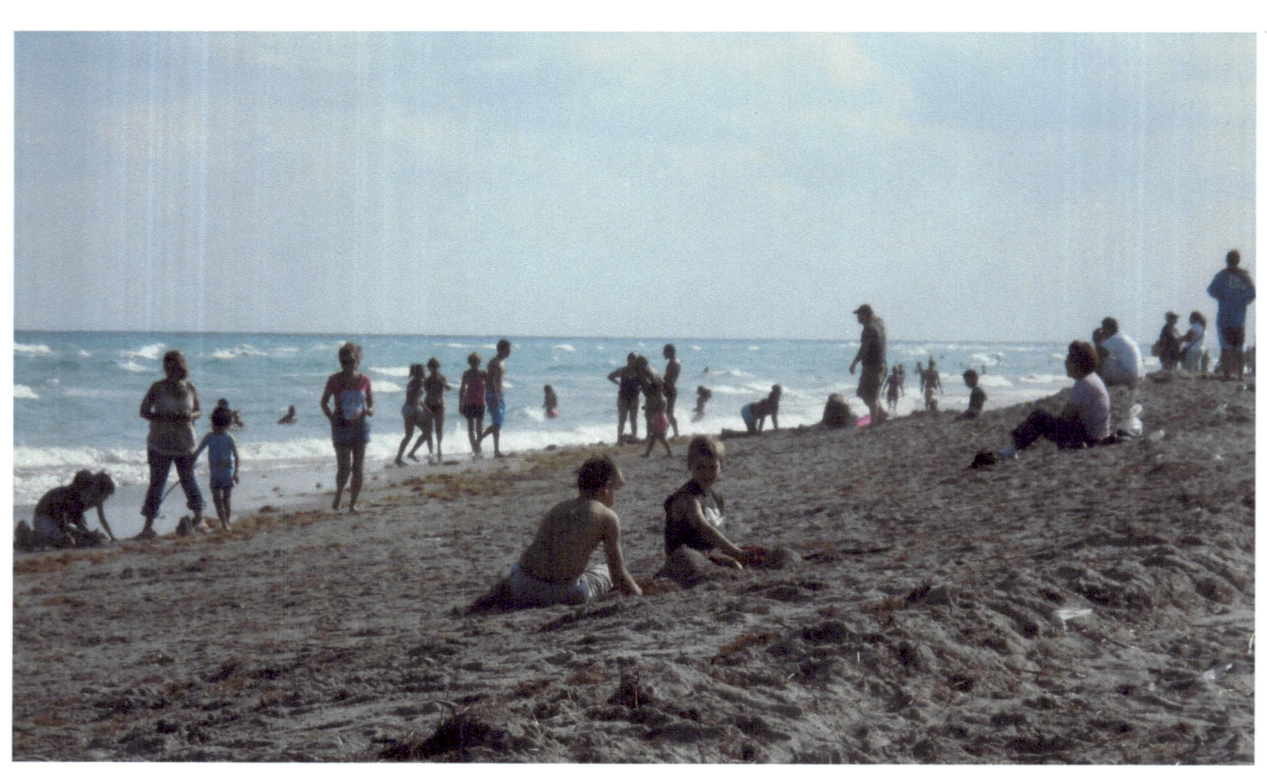

After storm.

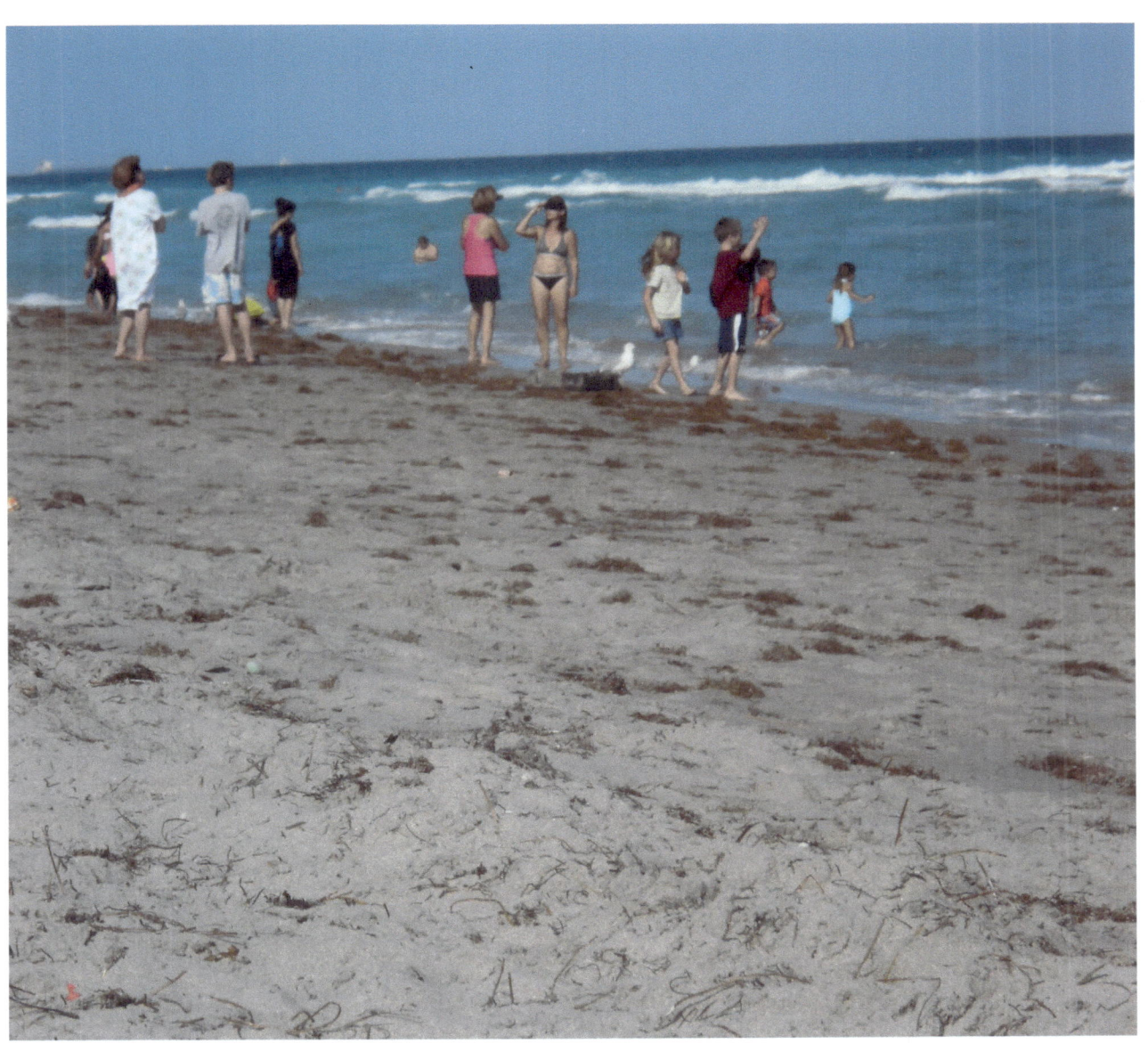

Anxiety on the beach after storm.

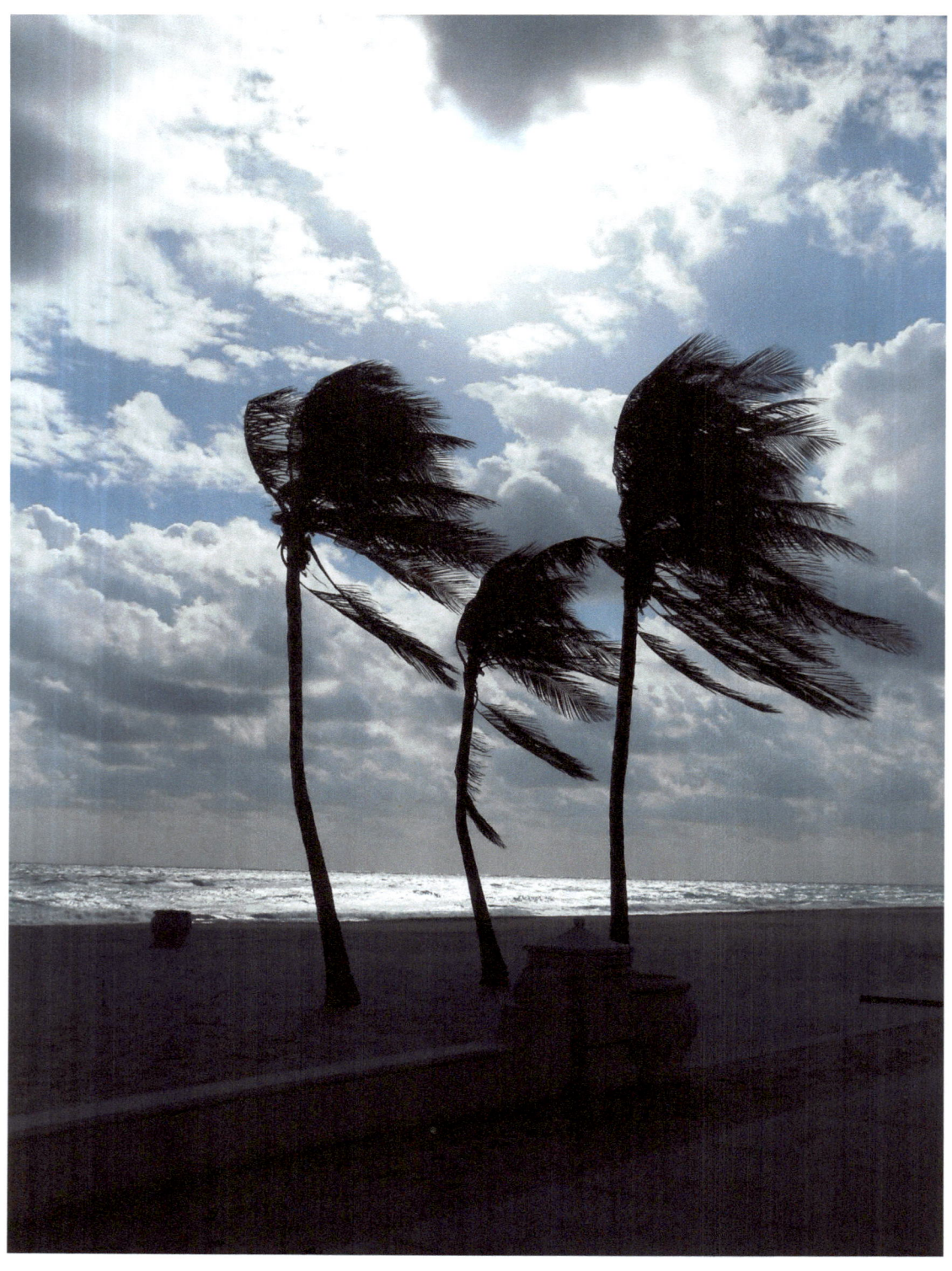

Windy.

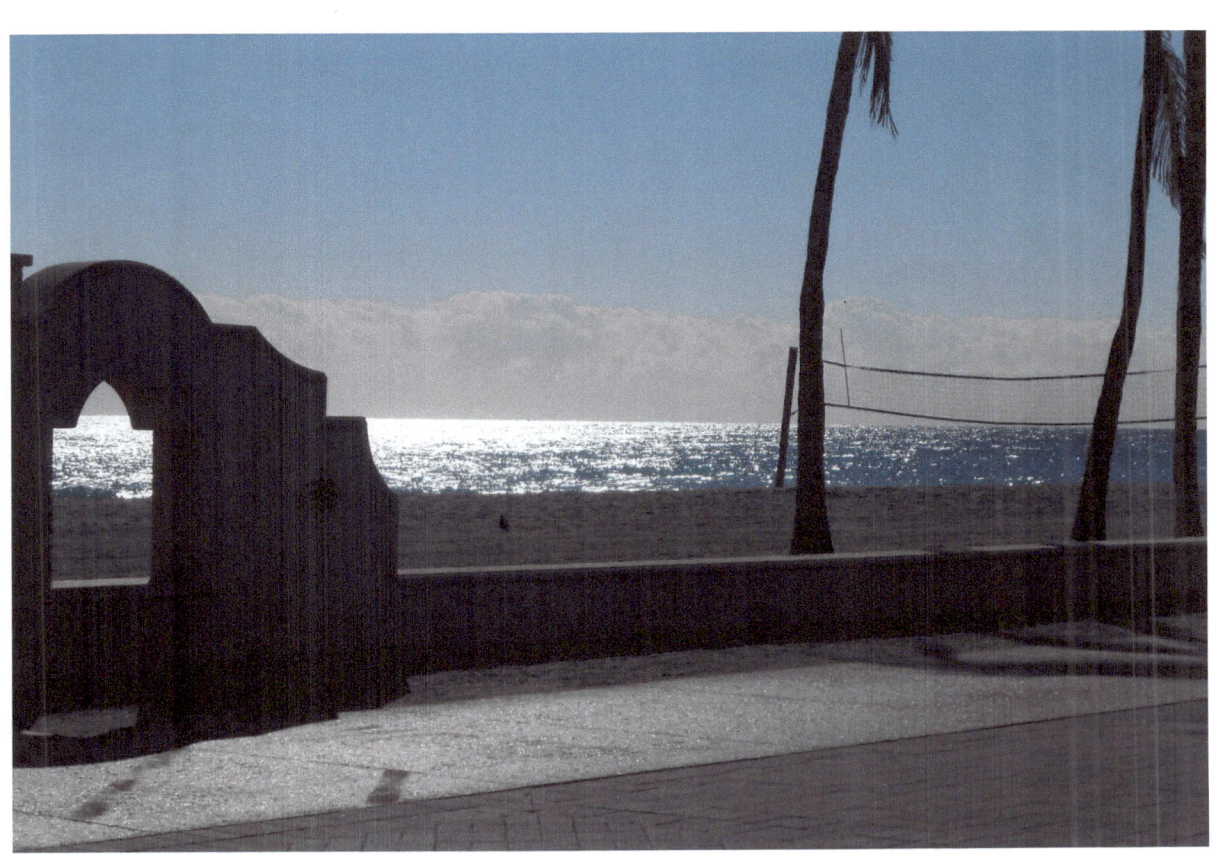

Quiet morning.

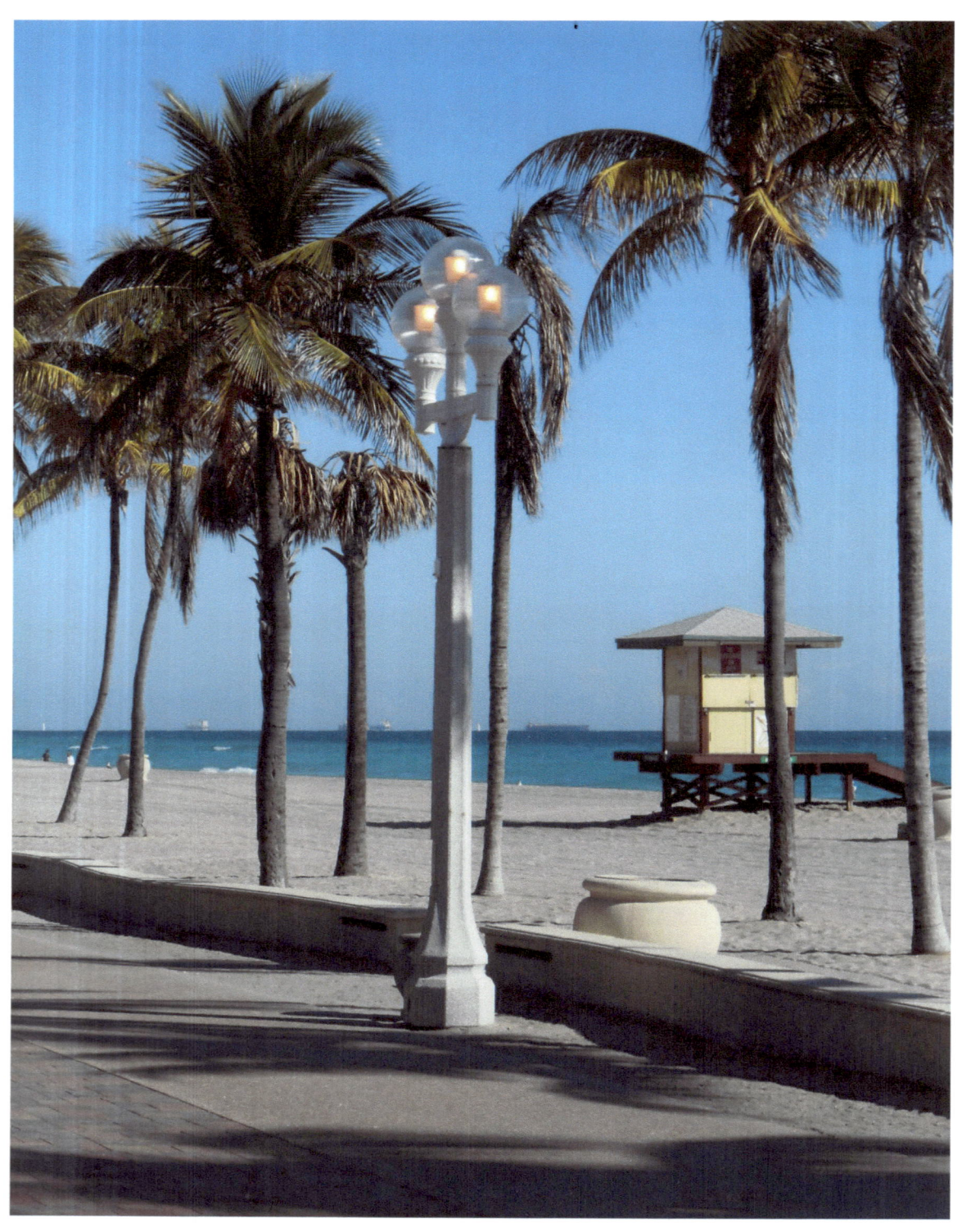

Morning beach.

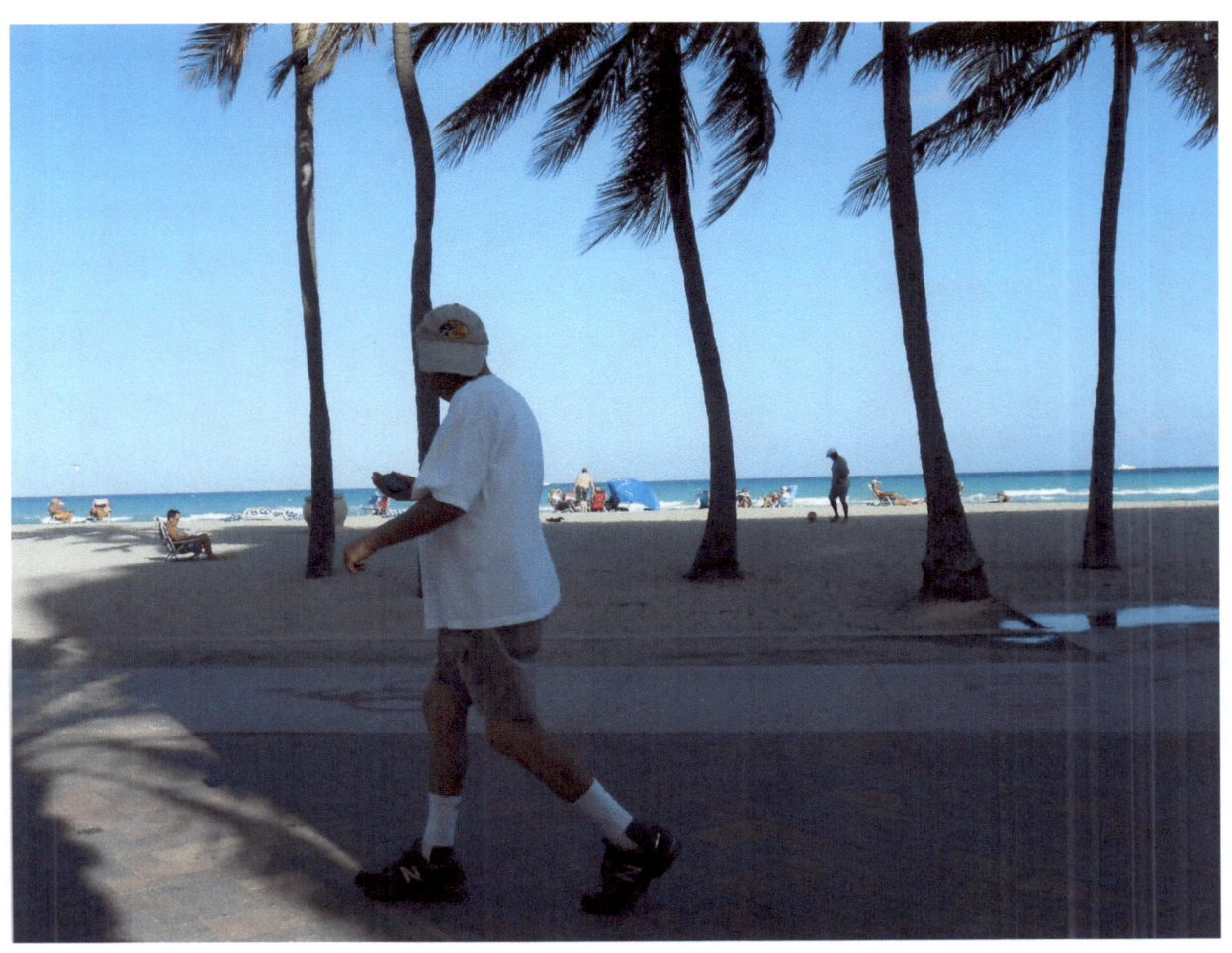

Getting in motion afternoon.

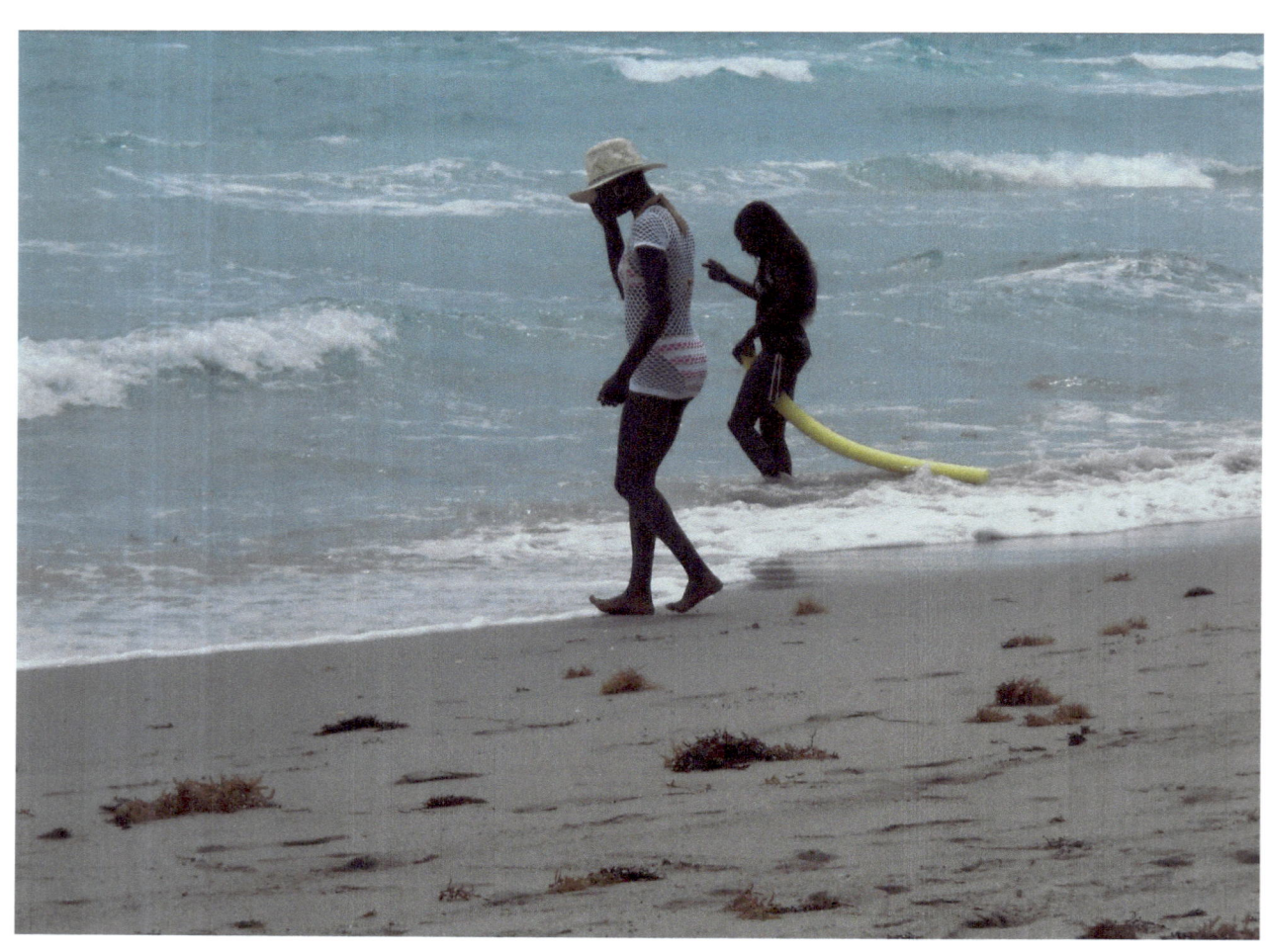

Just checking water.

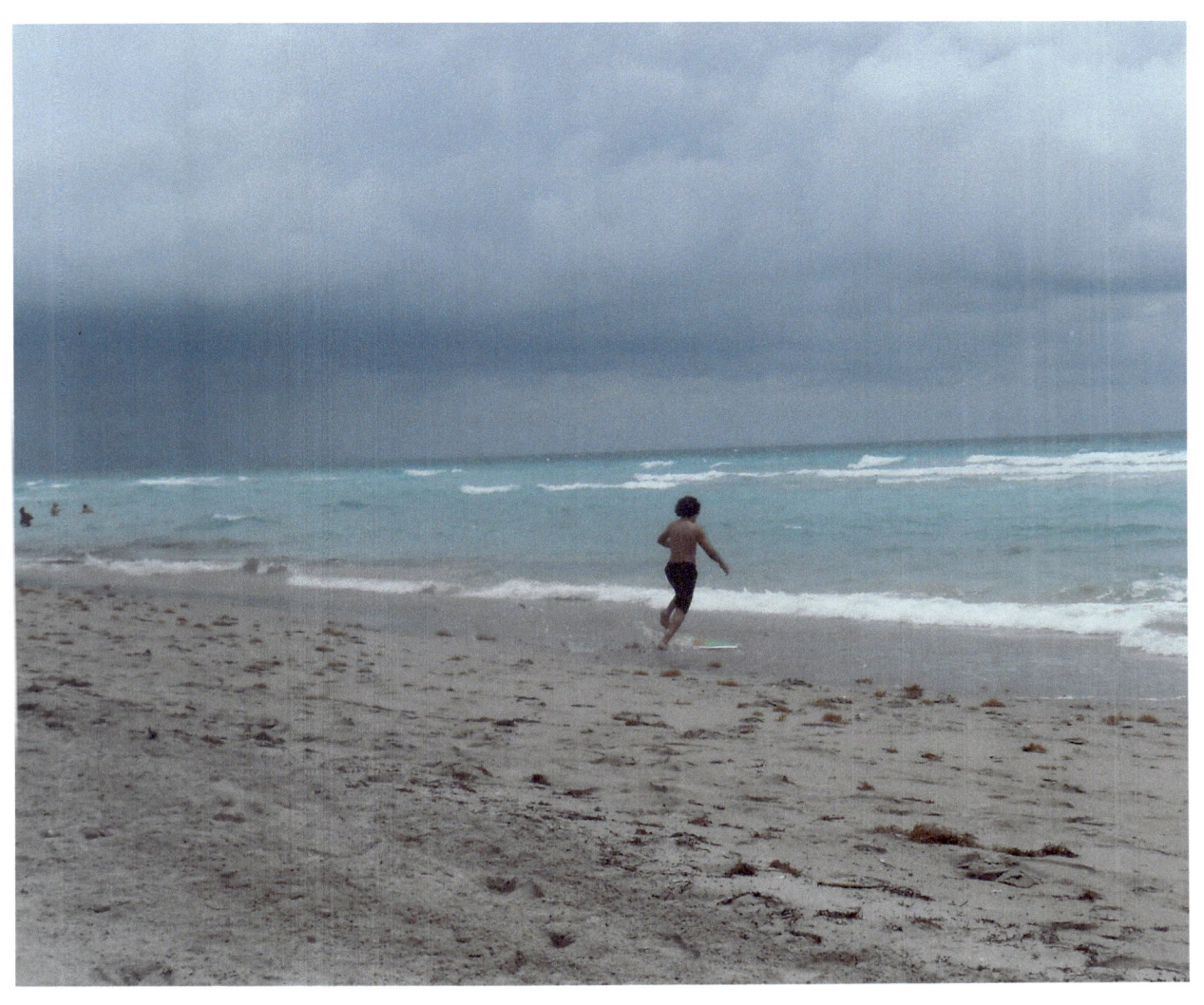

Learning to surf.

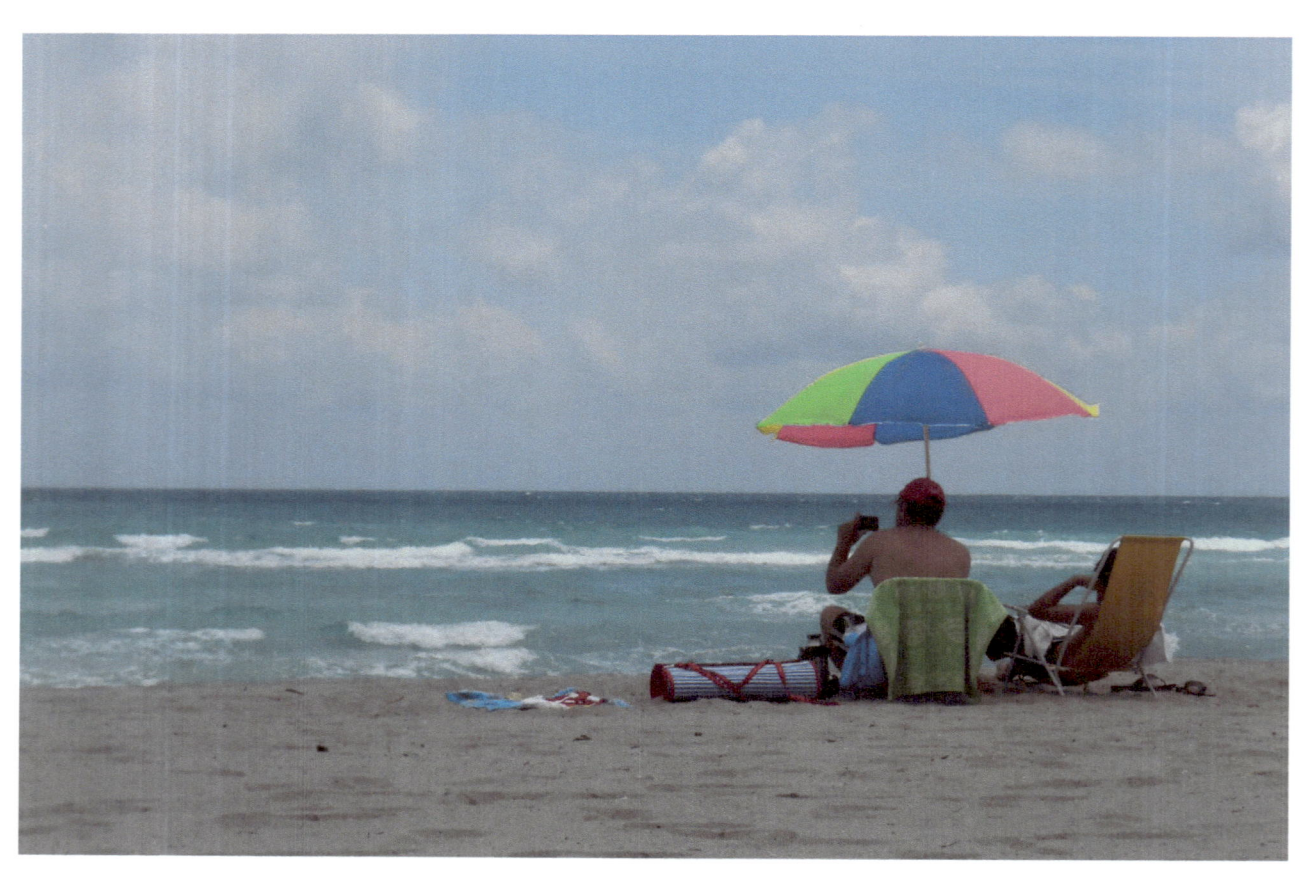

Capturing the Atlantic Ocean.

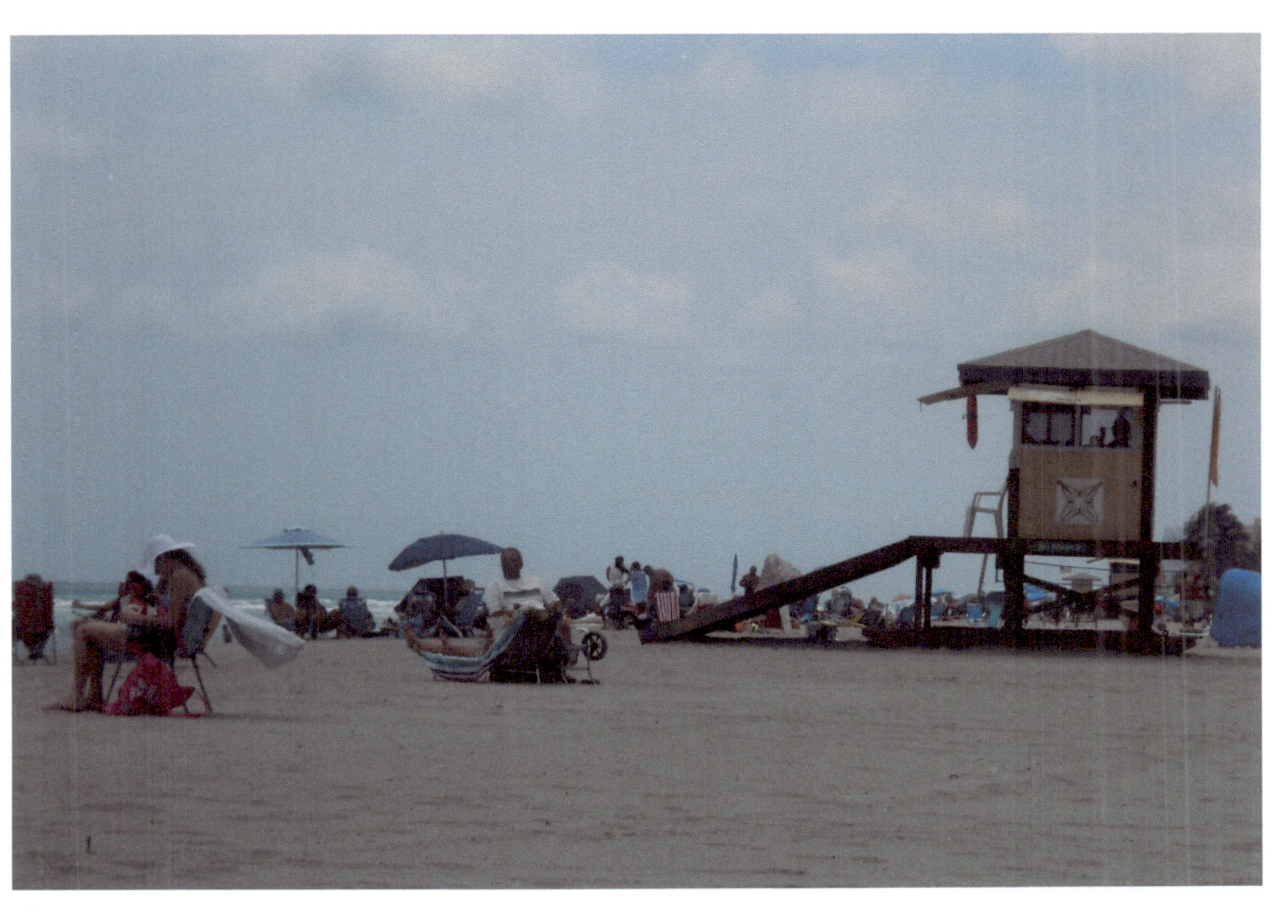

Another sunny day on the beach.

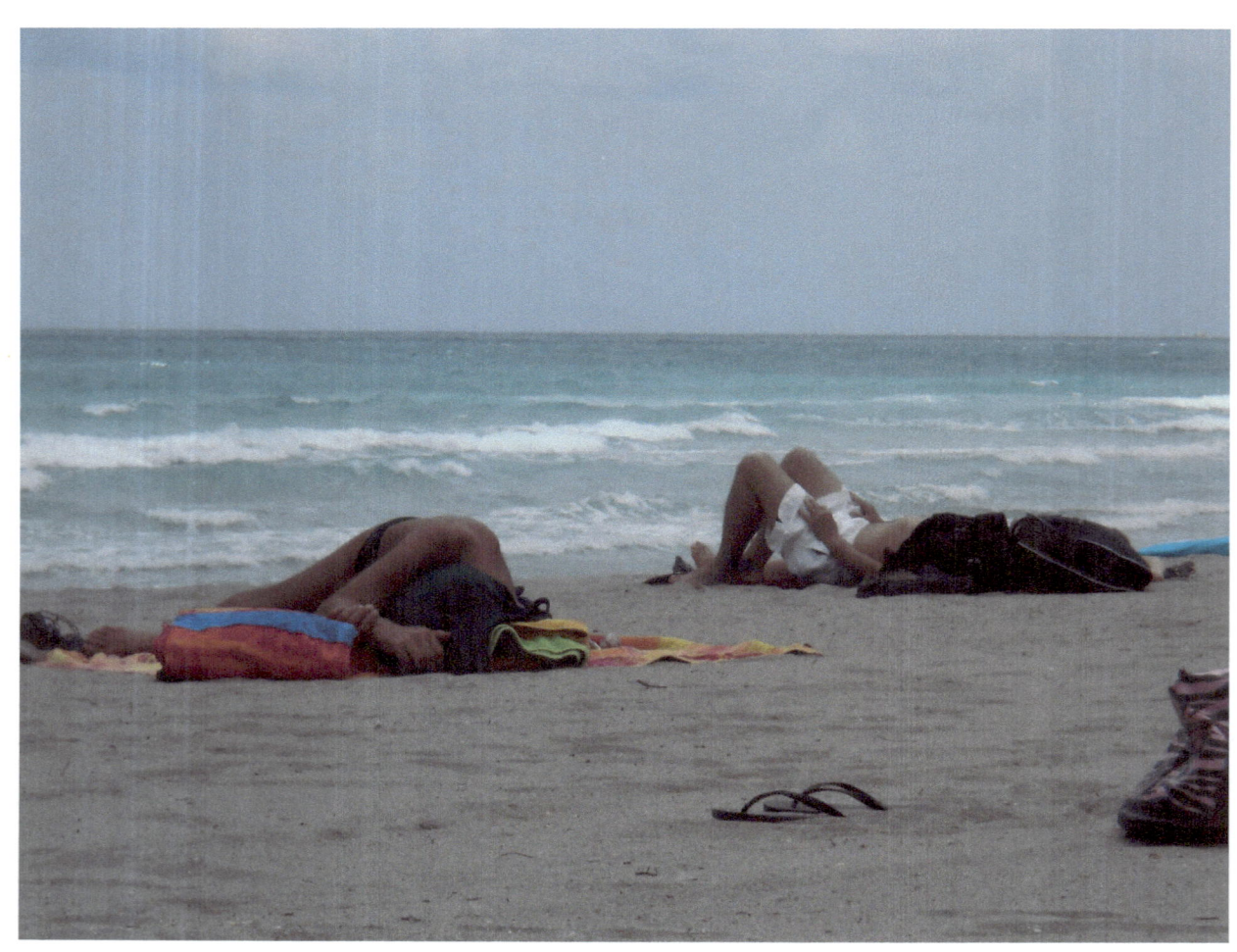

Sleeping with heads off.

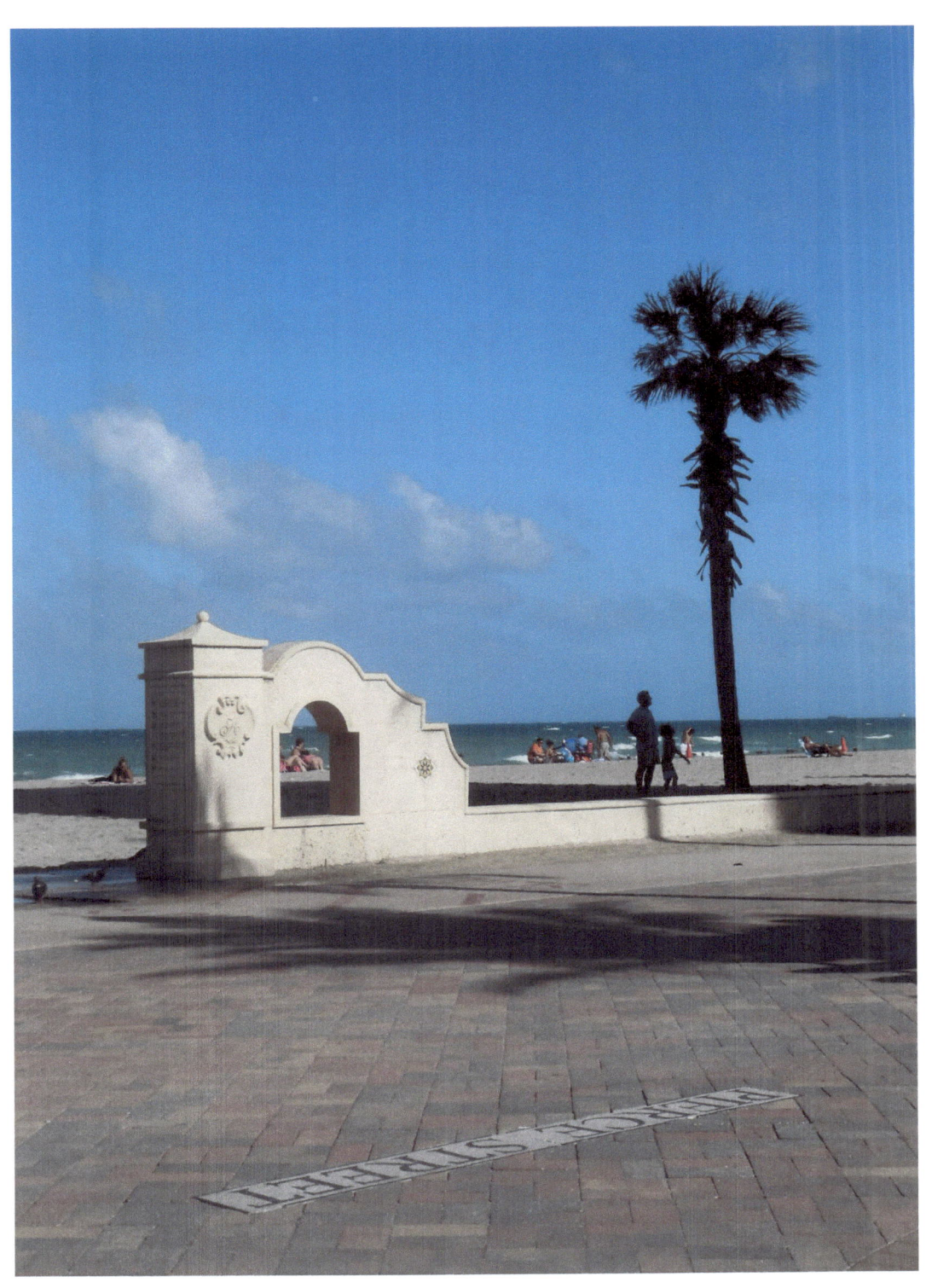

Pierce street & Broadwalk.

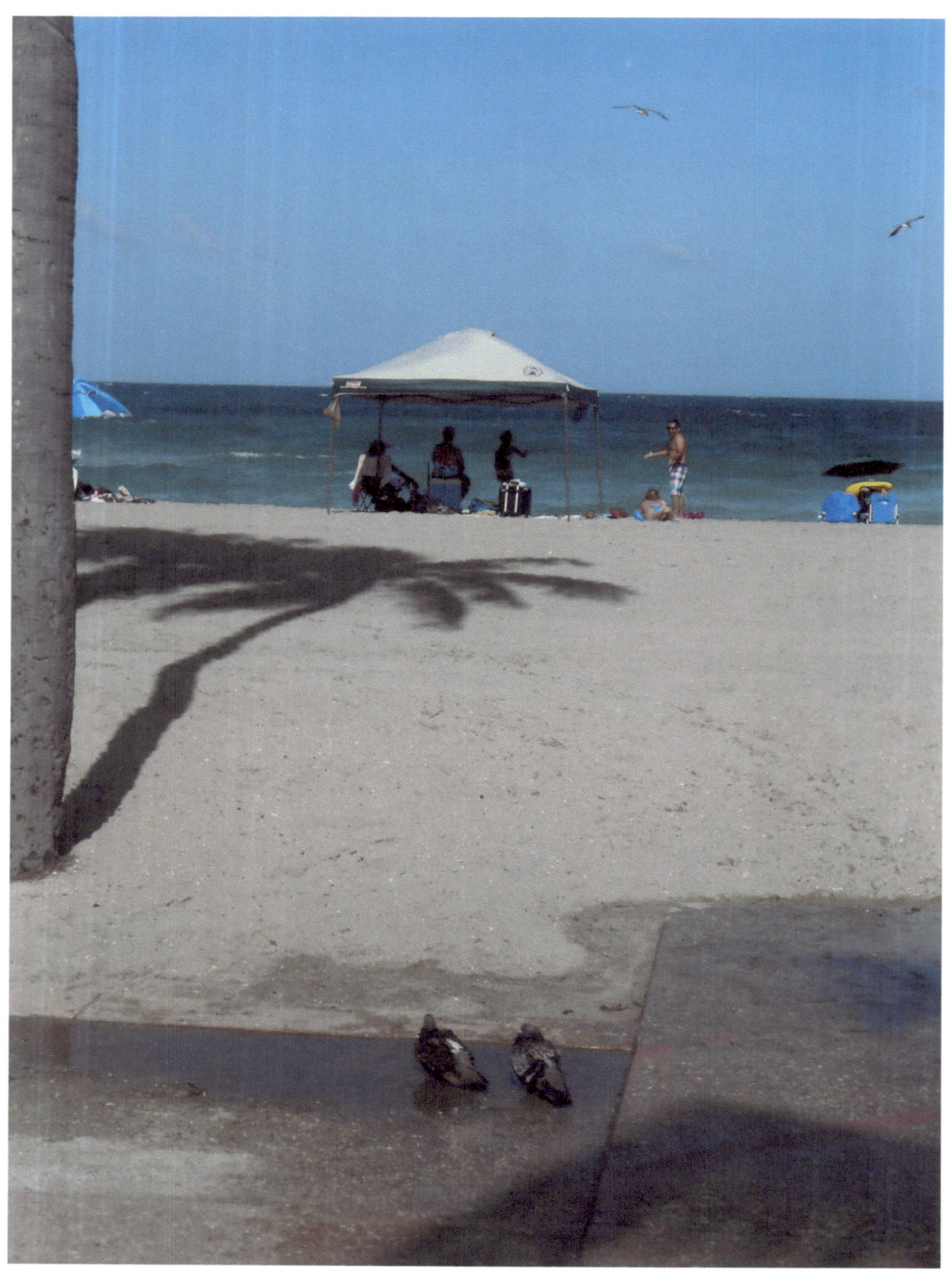

The beards.

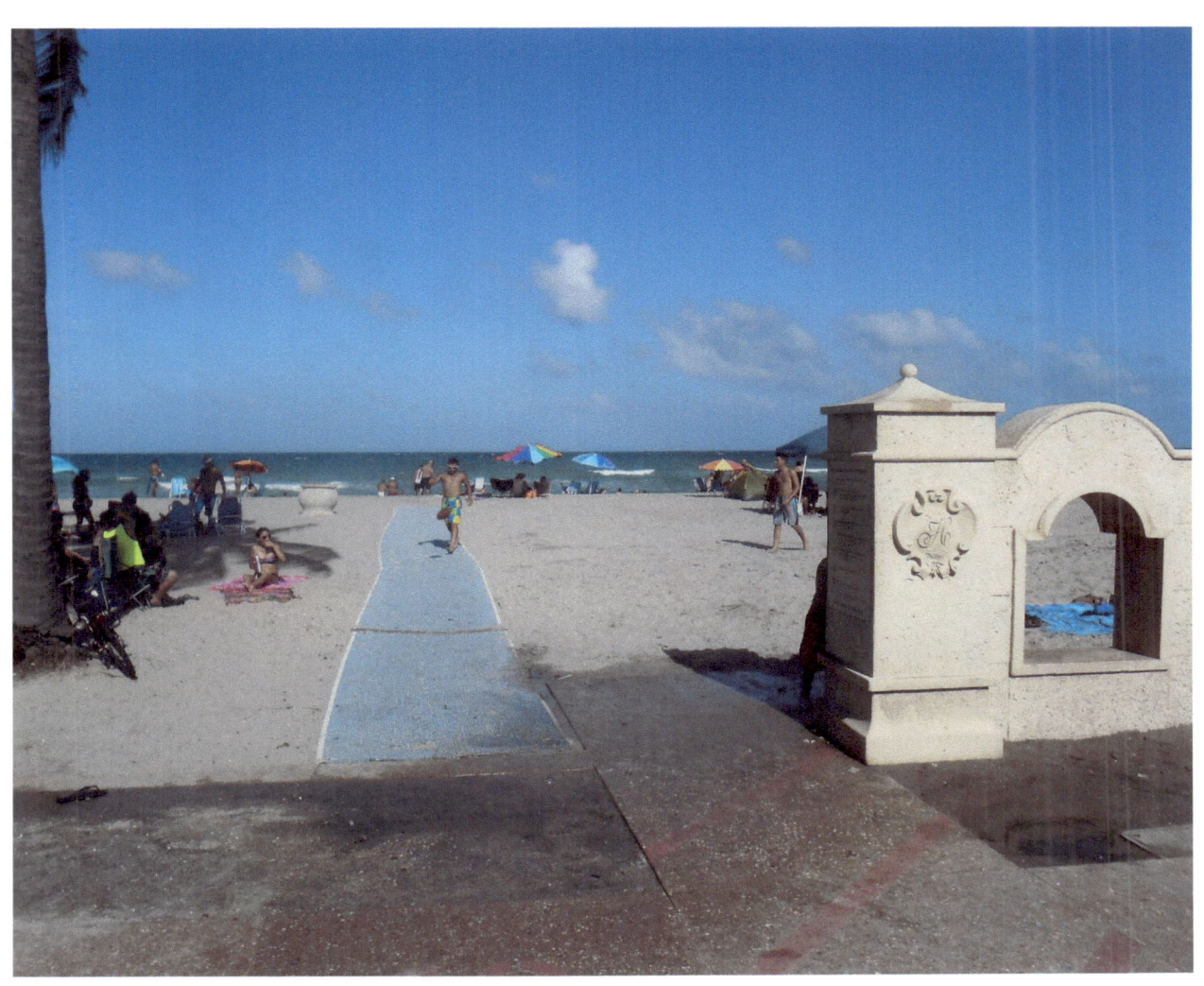

The road to Paradise.

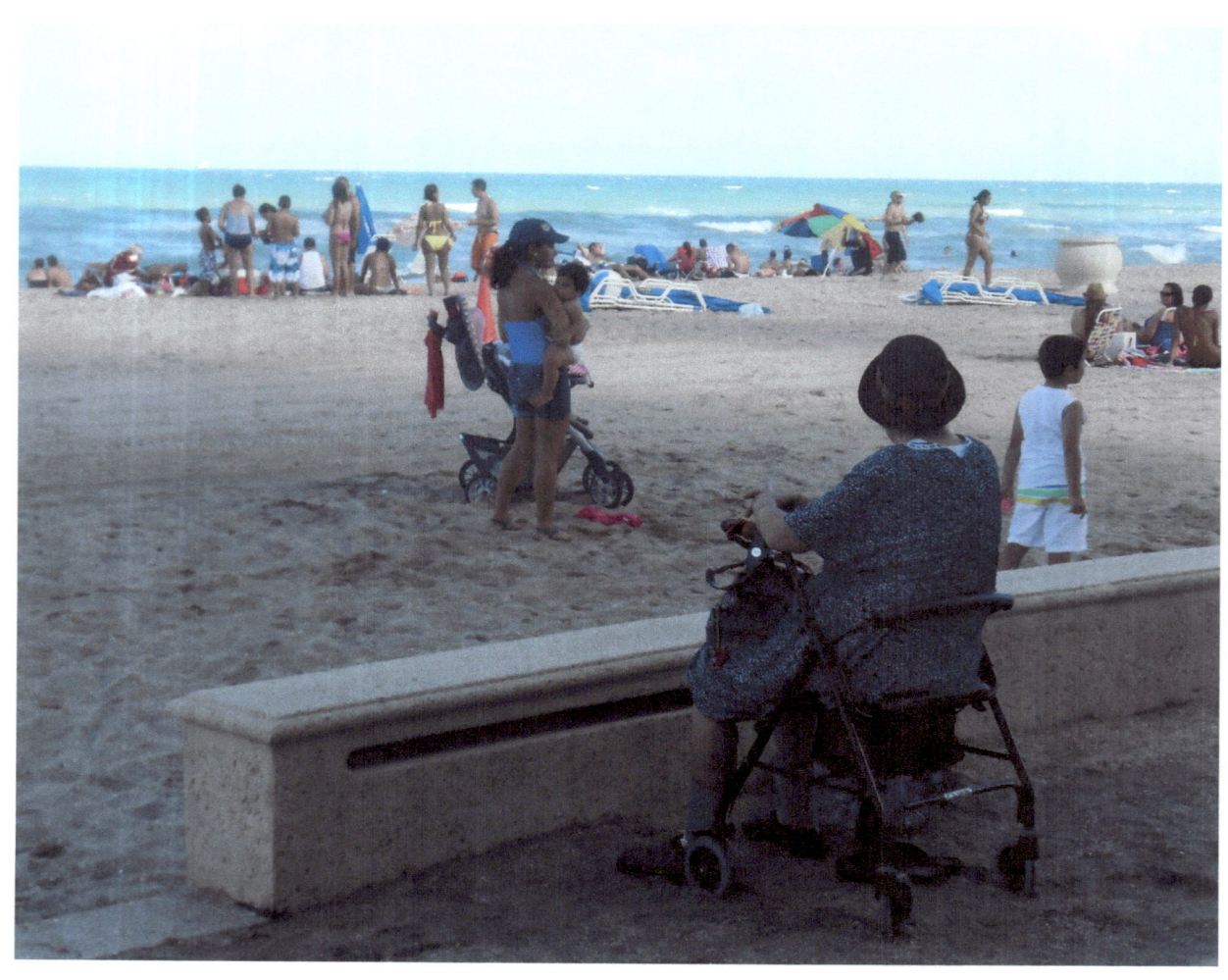

Time is the essence.

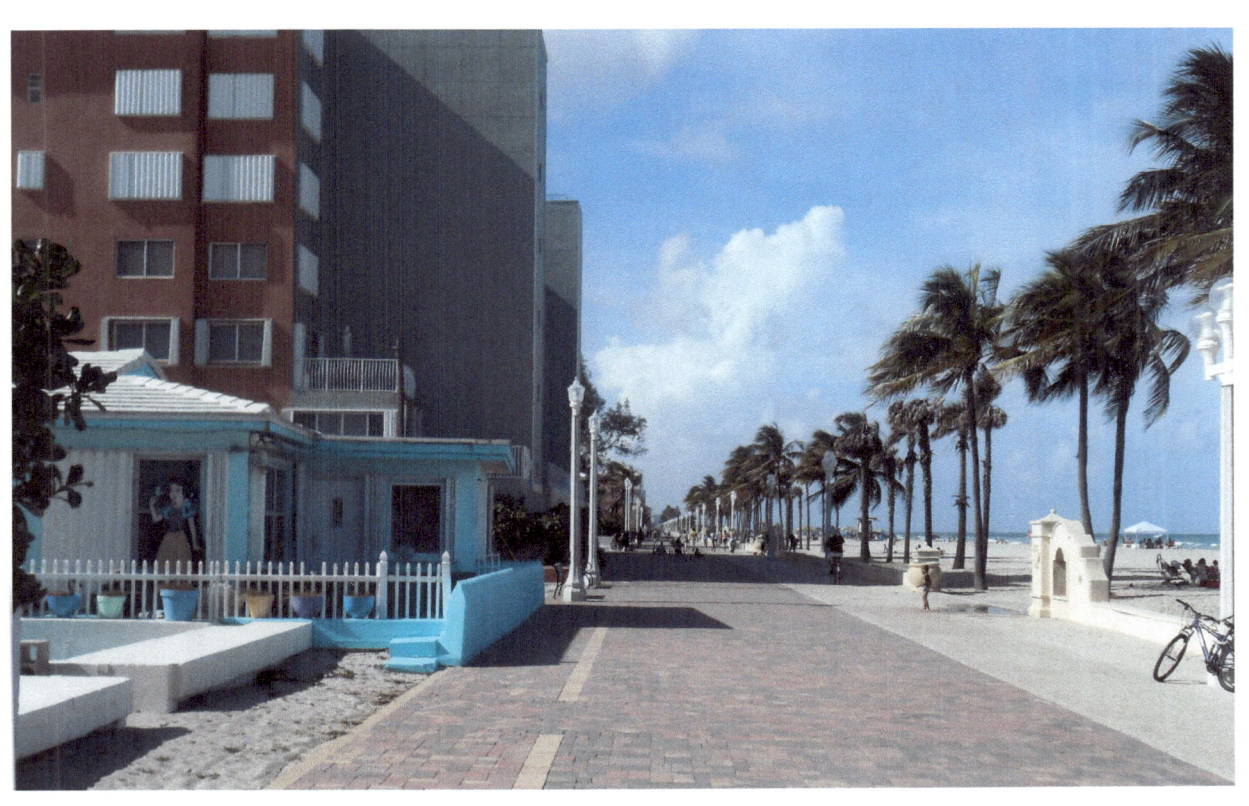

Windy afternoon.

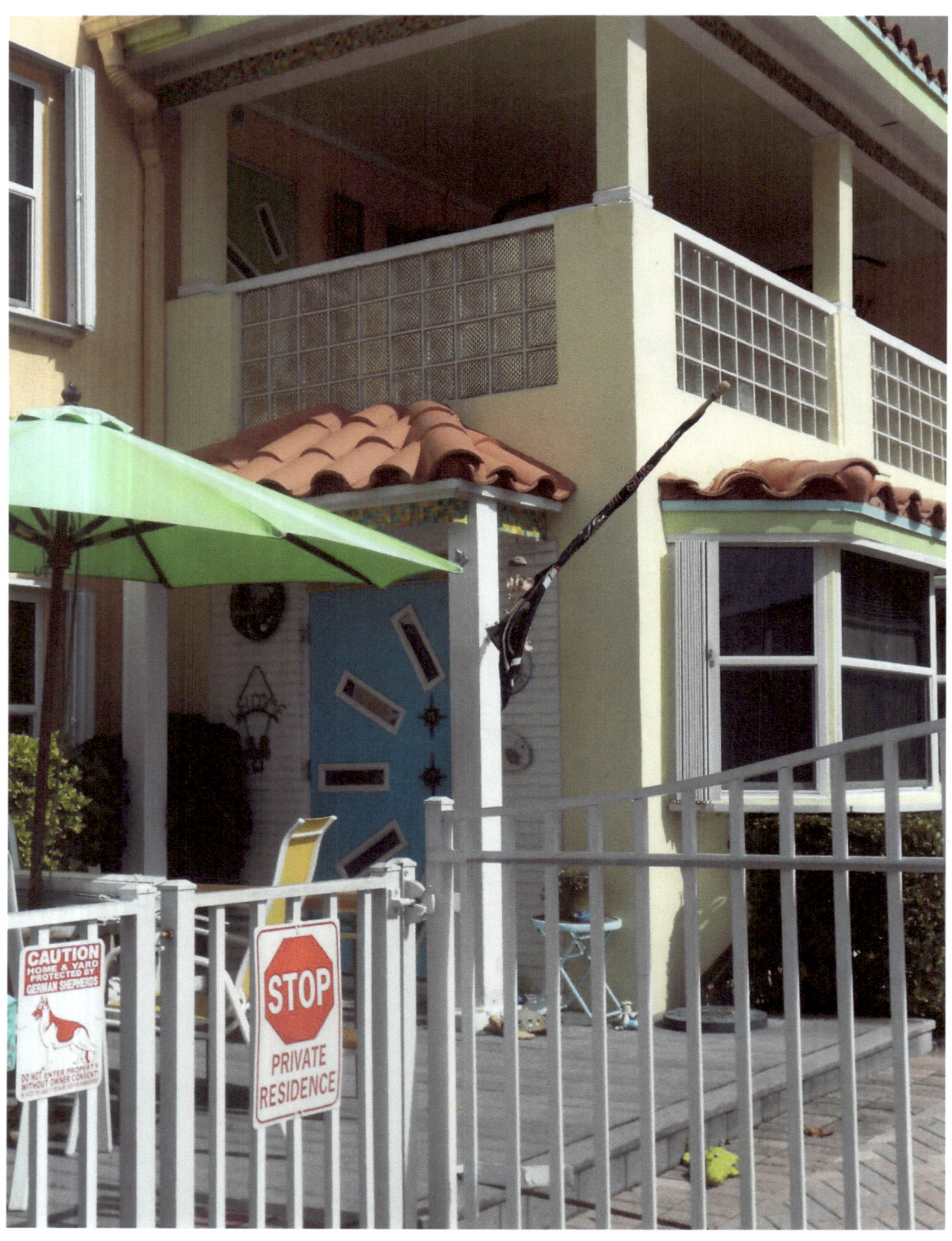

Living near Broadwalk at Arizona street, in a house where movies have been made.

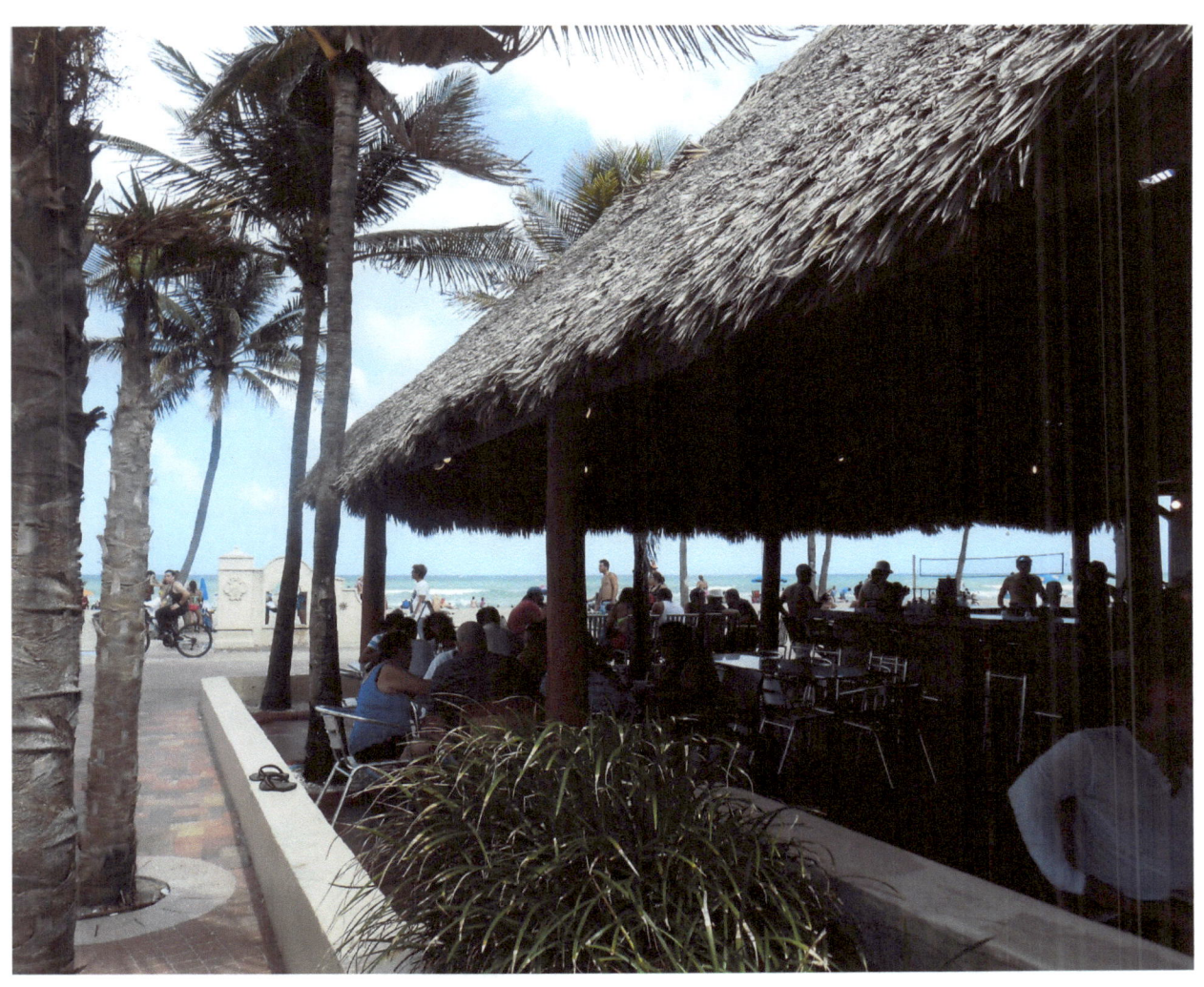

Eating at Broadwalk.

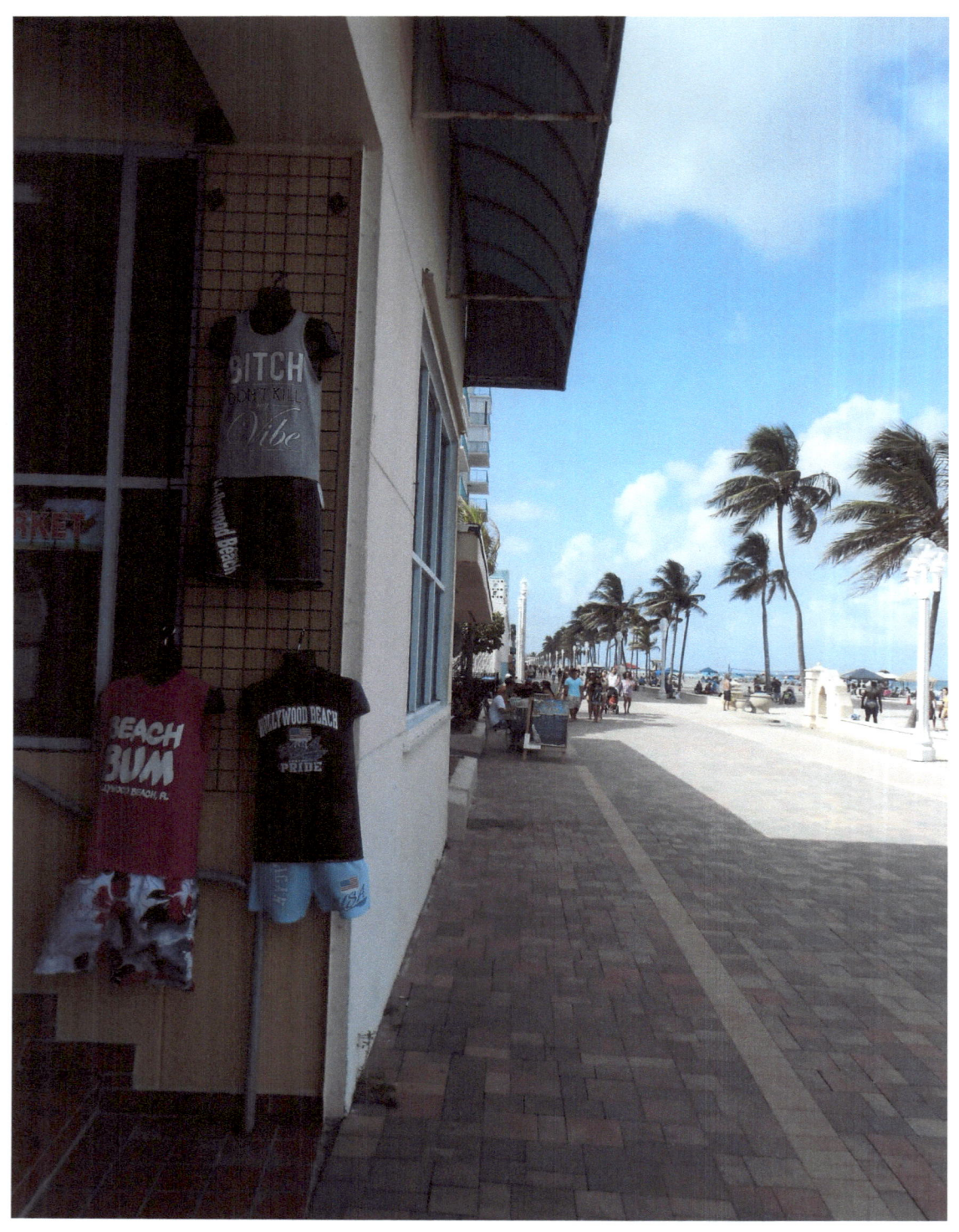

Shopping for t-shirts at Broadwalk.

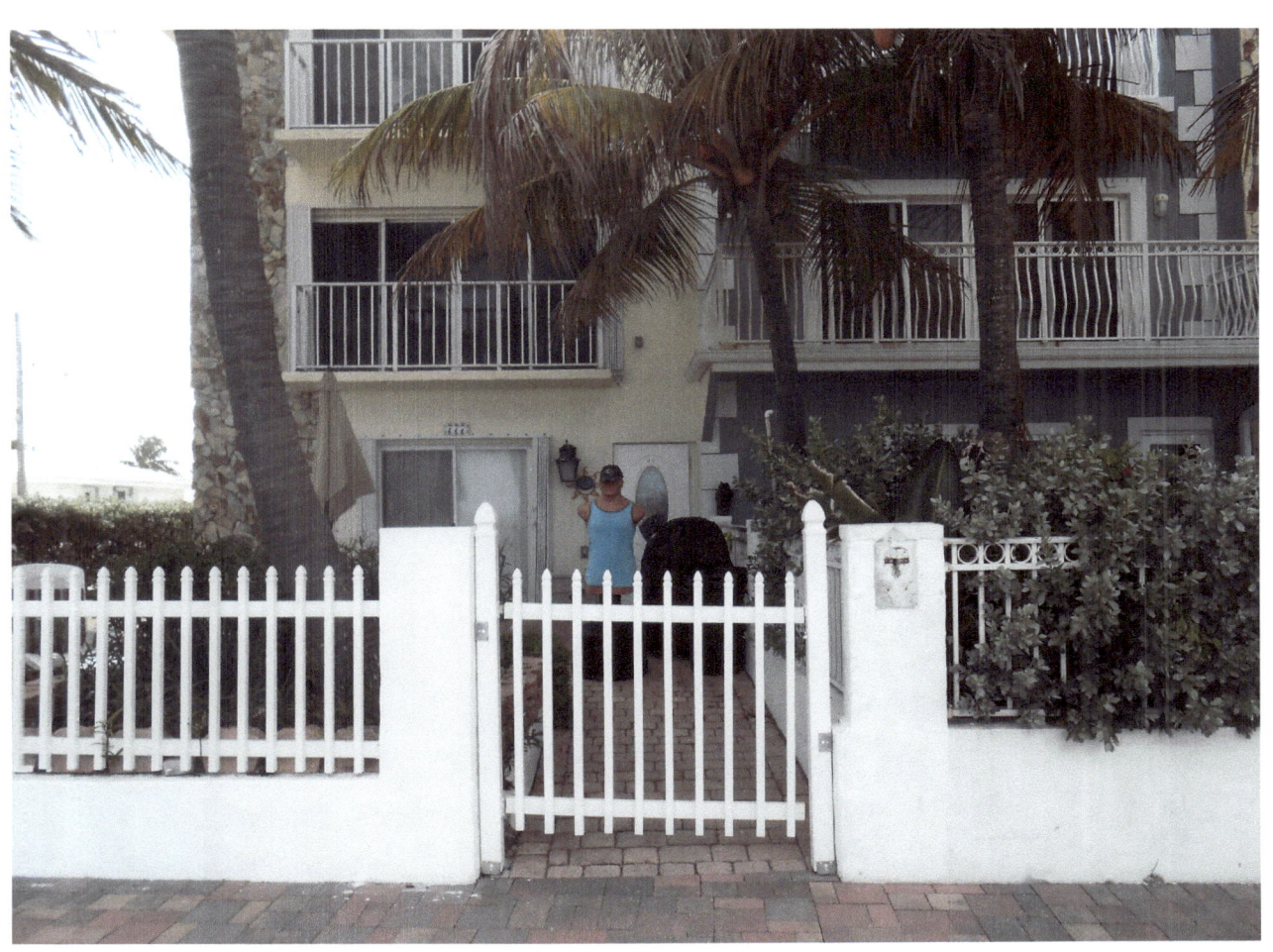

The guard.

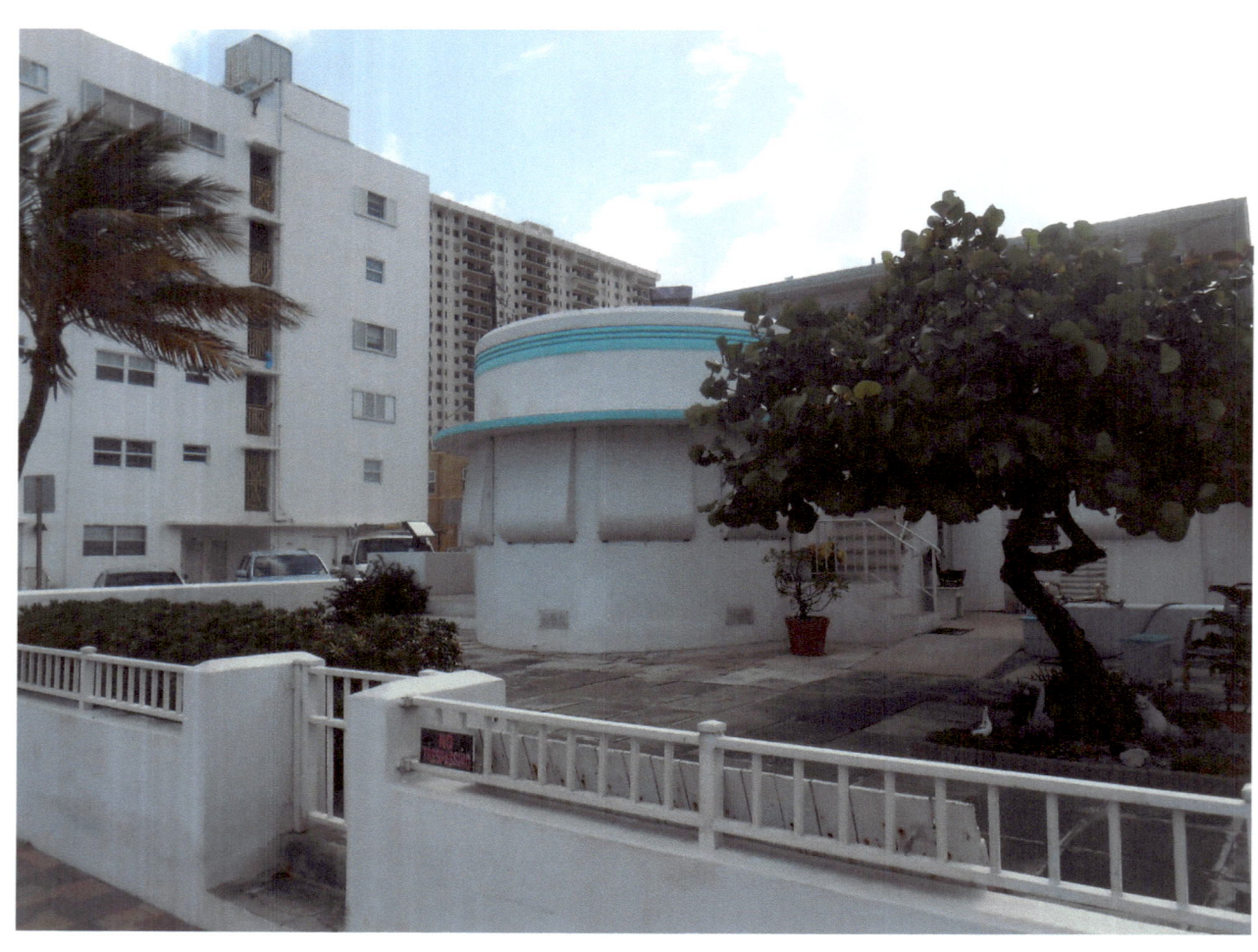

Another small, fanciful and quiet house on Hollywood Beach Broadwalk.

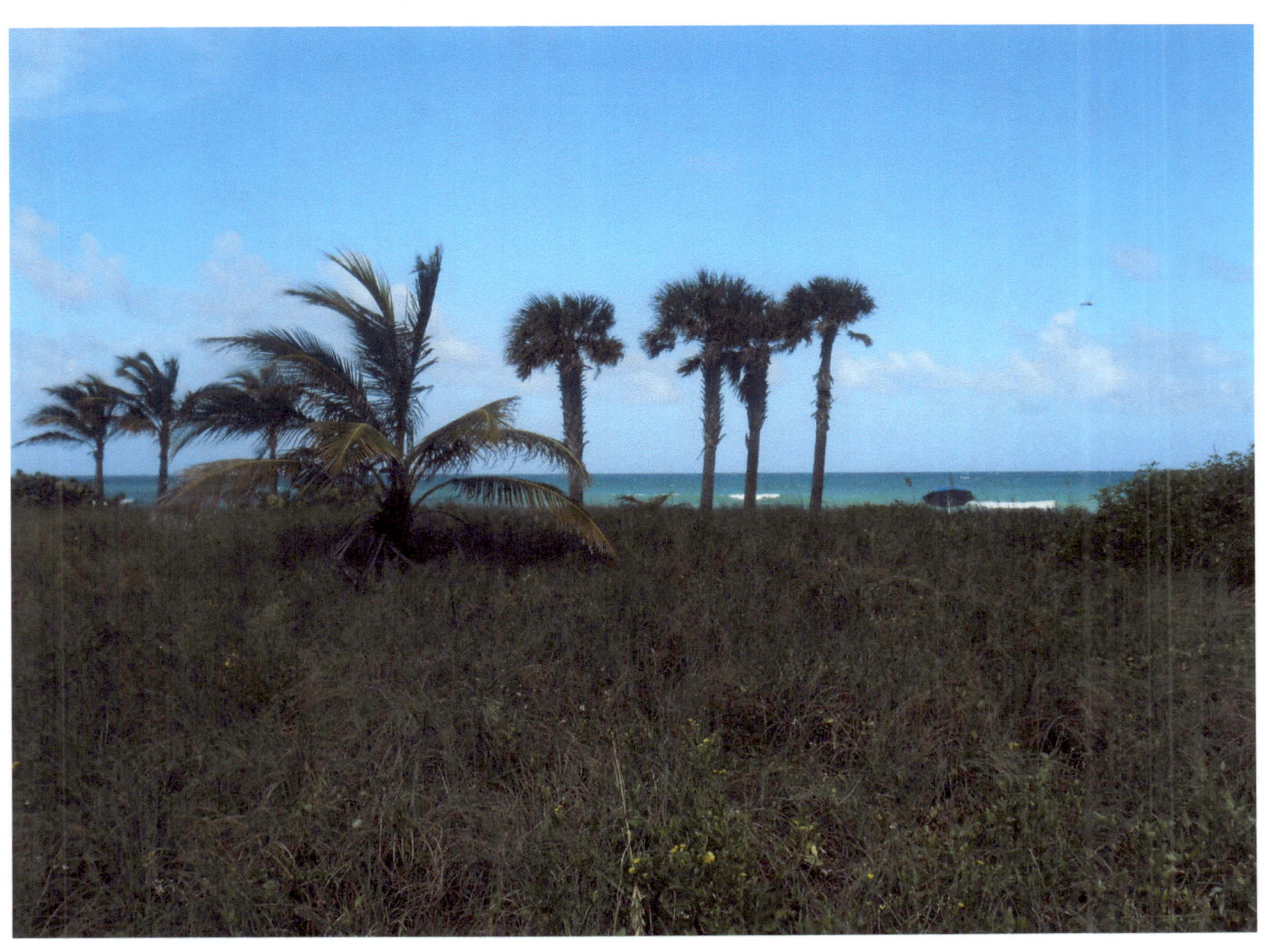

Wild nature.

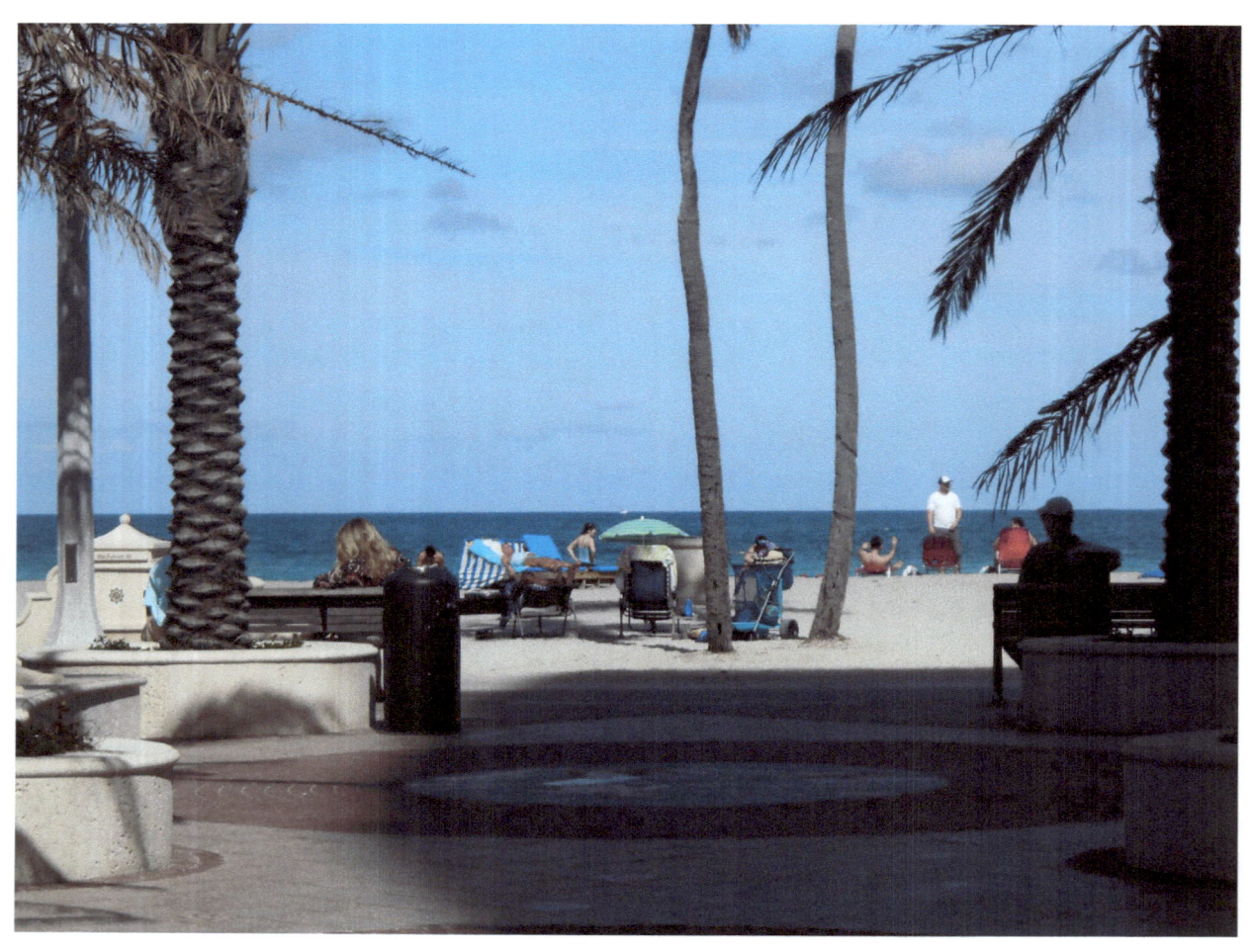

Tranquility.

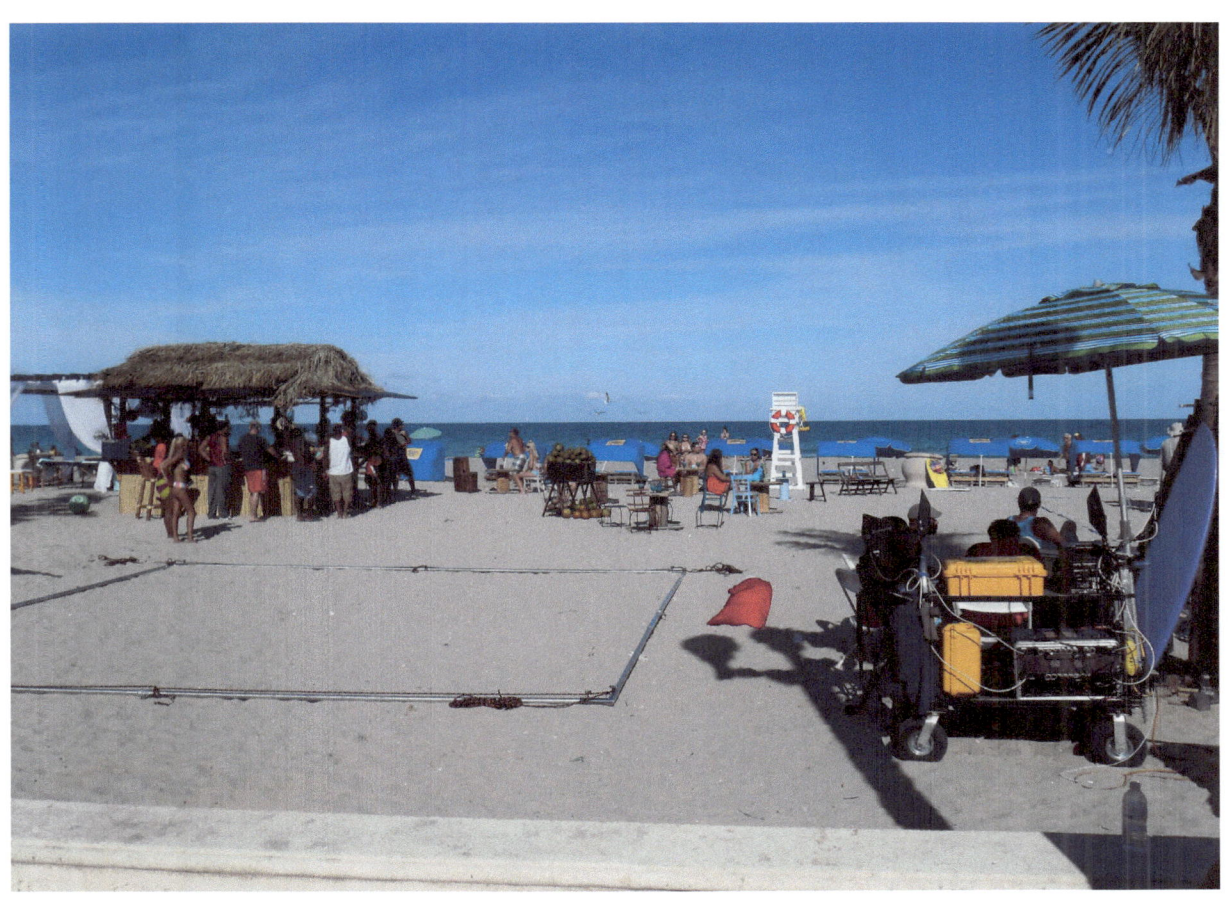

Often, the famous Hollywood moviemakers create California's scenes in Hollywood, Florida. Also, many scenes of the TV series "Grace Land" have been made on Broadwalk.

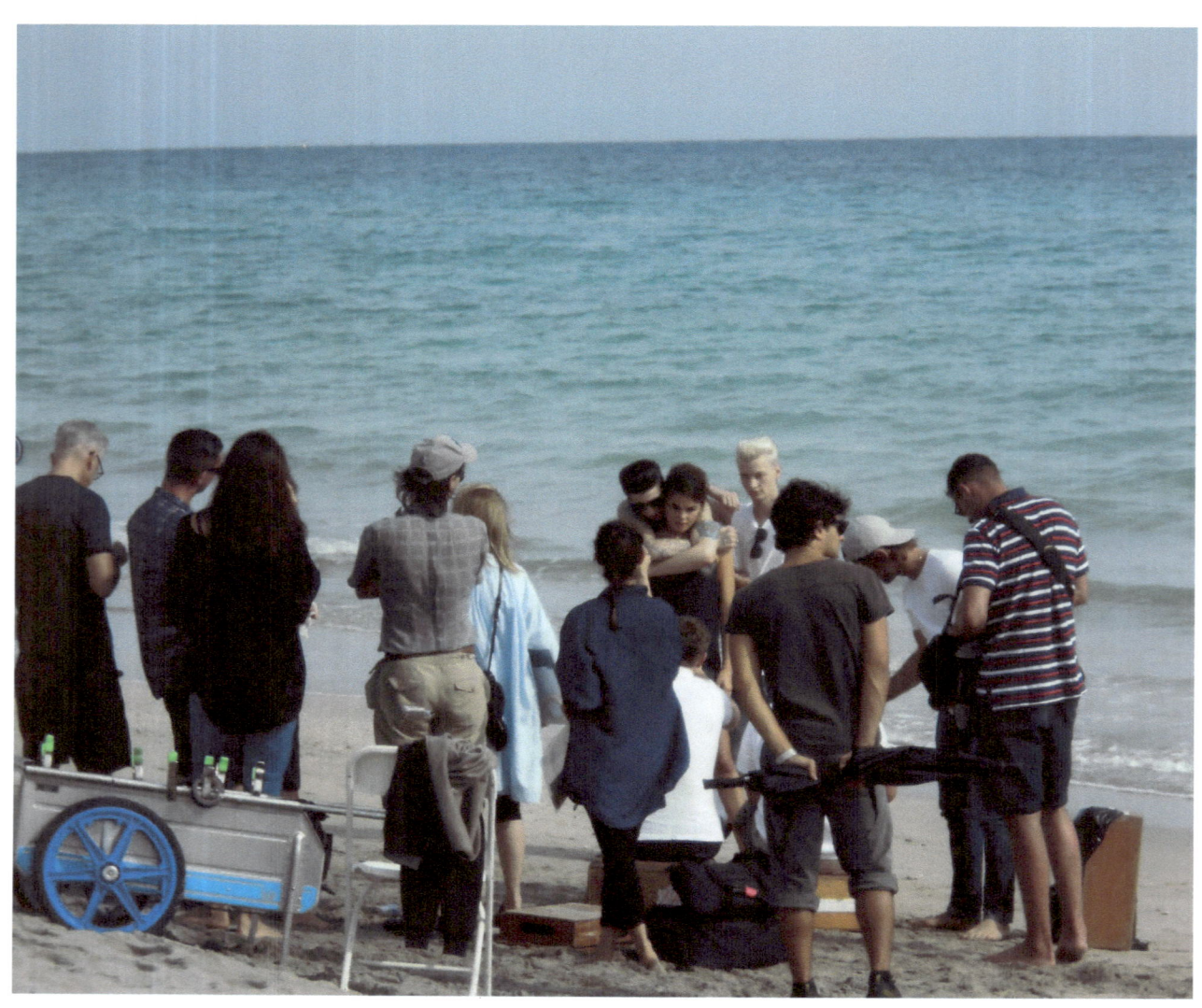

Hollywood beach is a favorite location for the fashion shots.

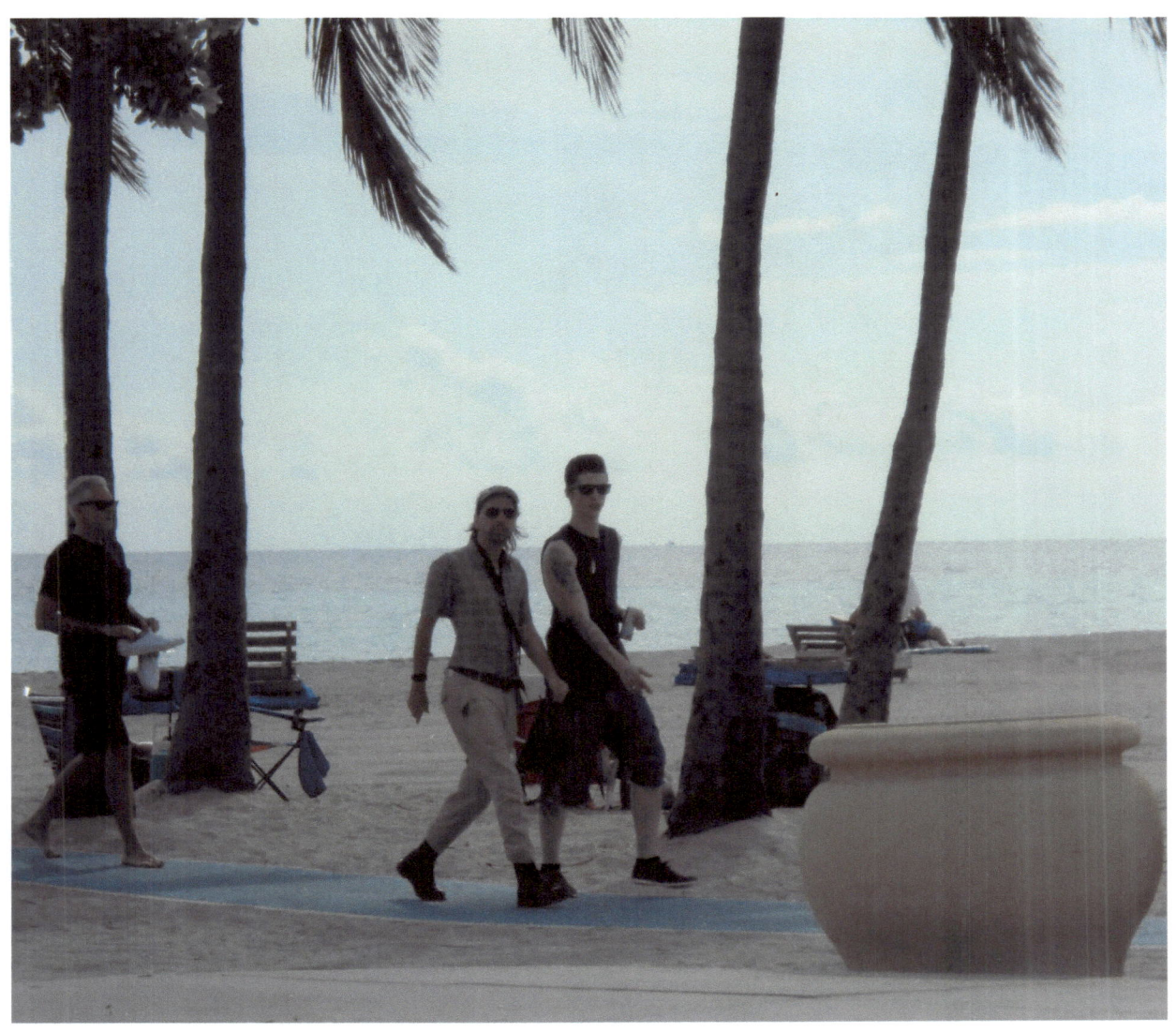

The work is over.

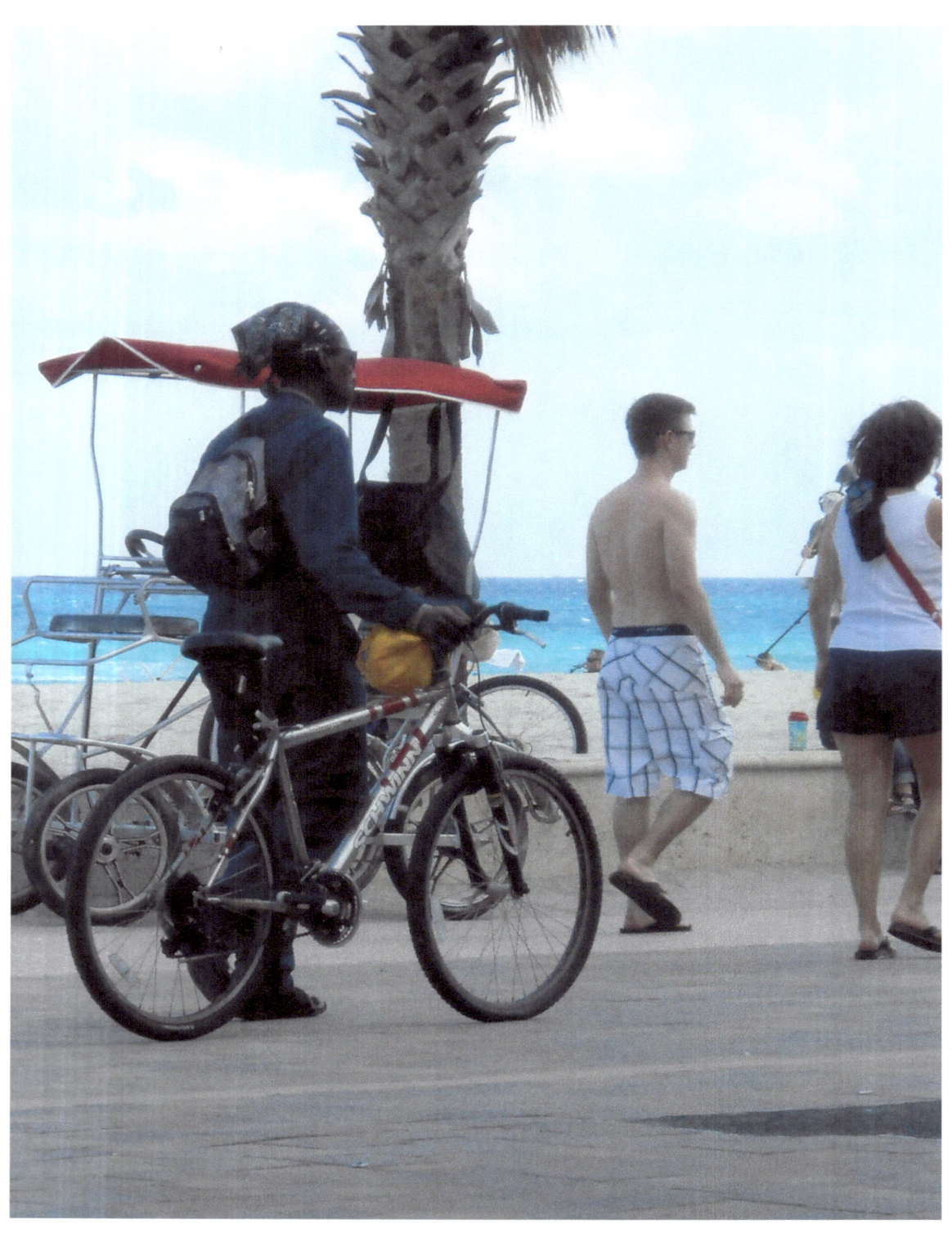

Another beautiful day in Hollywood.

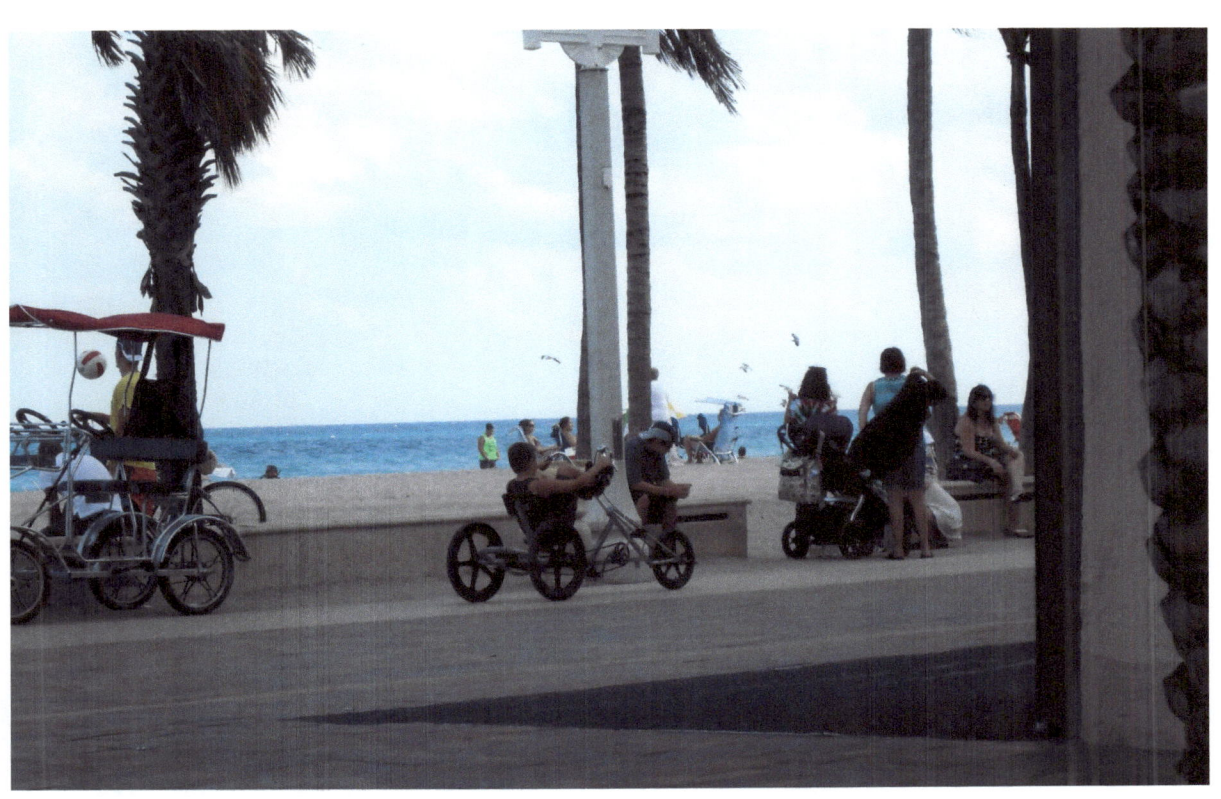

Having a great time.

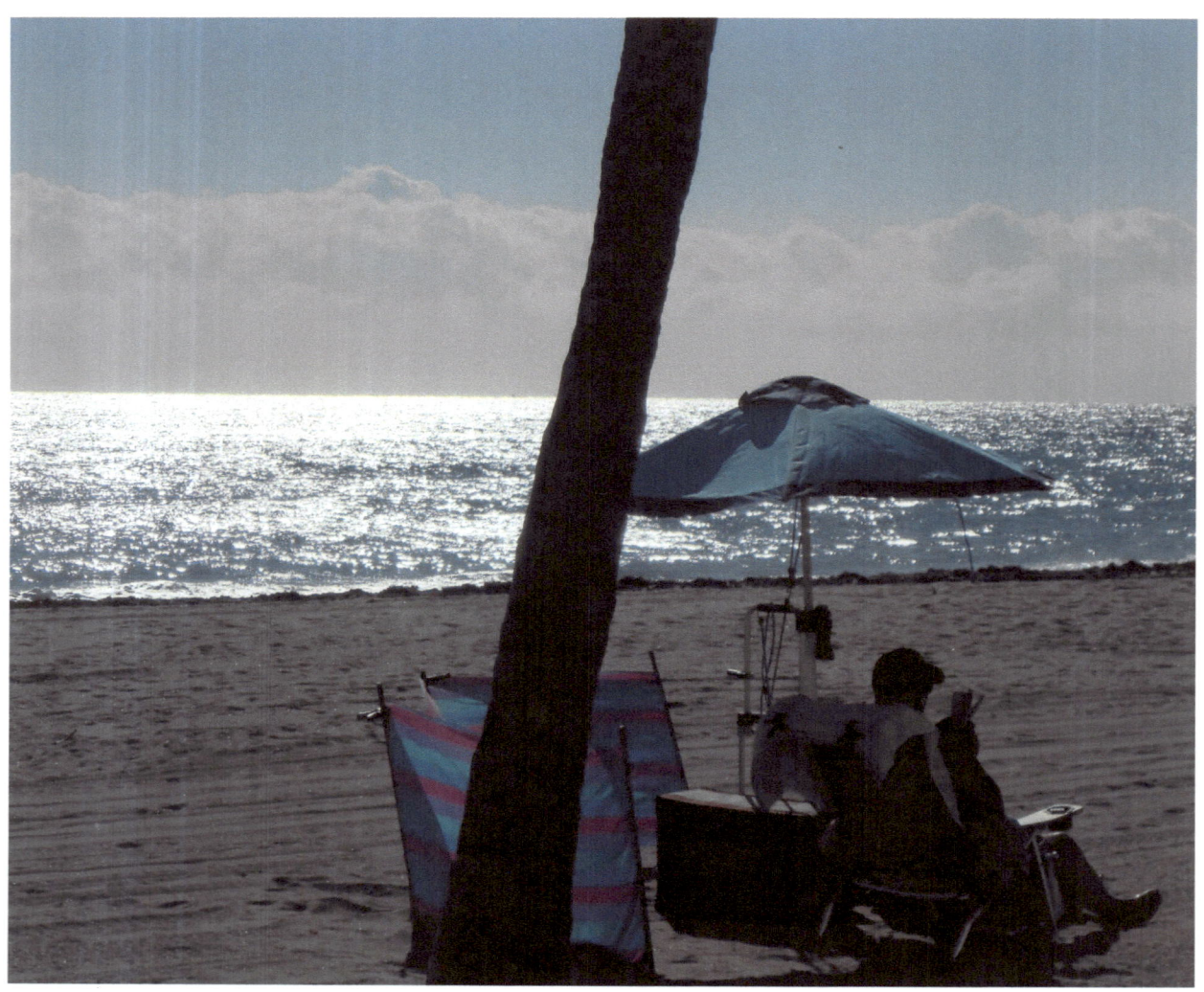

The beach.

HOLLYWOOD BROADWALK: FLORIDIAN PARADISE

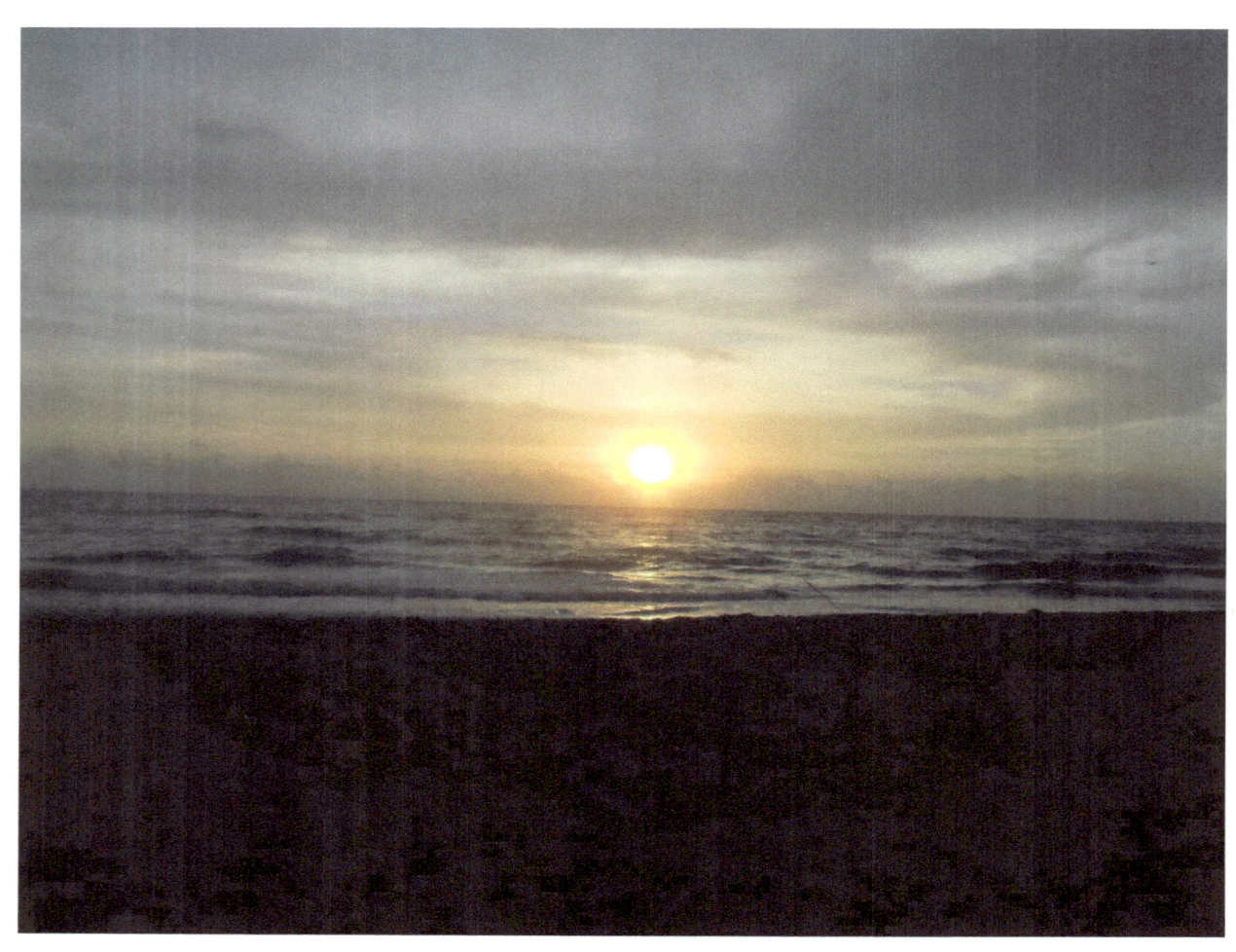

Sunrise on Broadwalk.

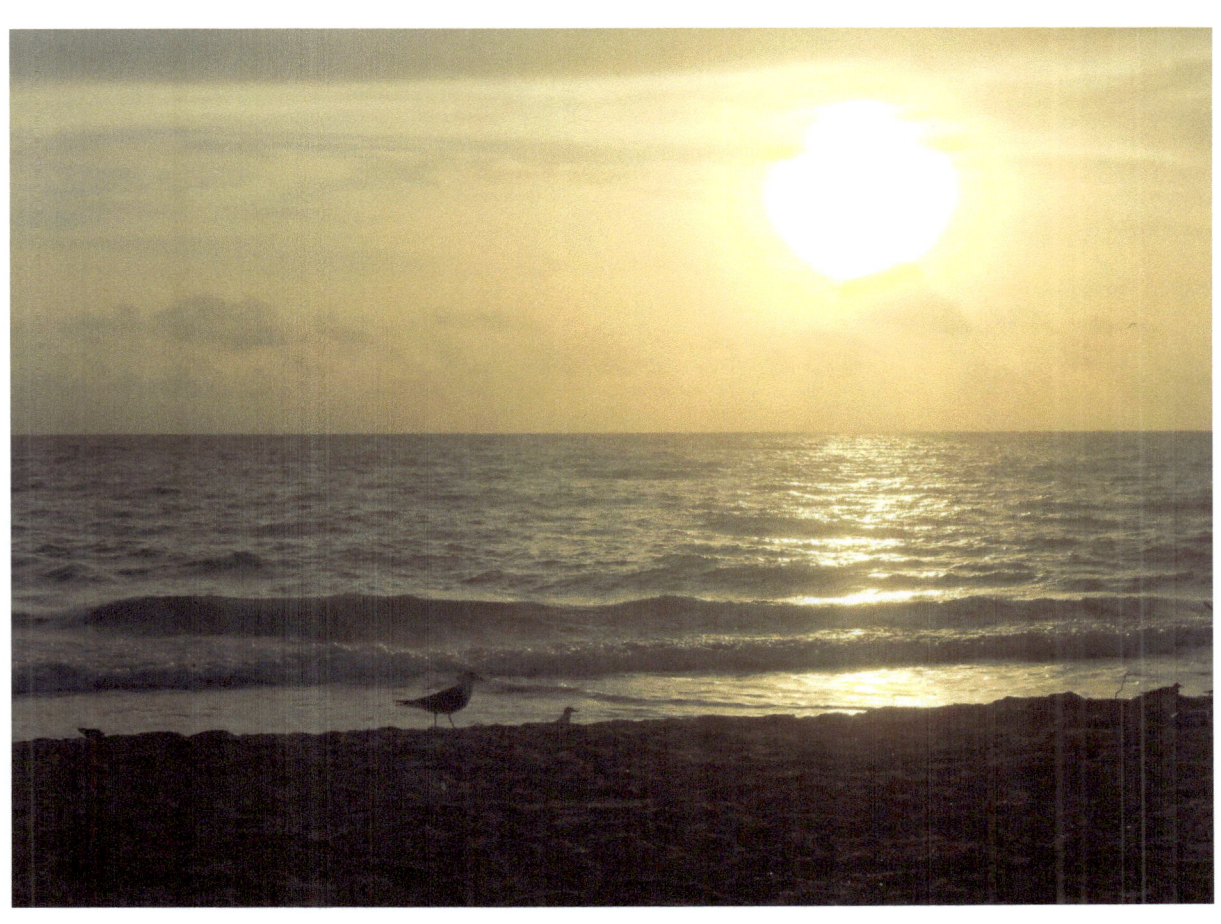

Another morning on the beach in Hollywood, Florida.

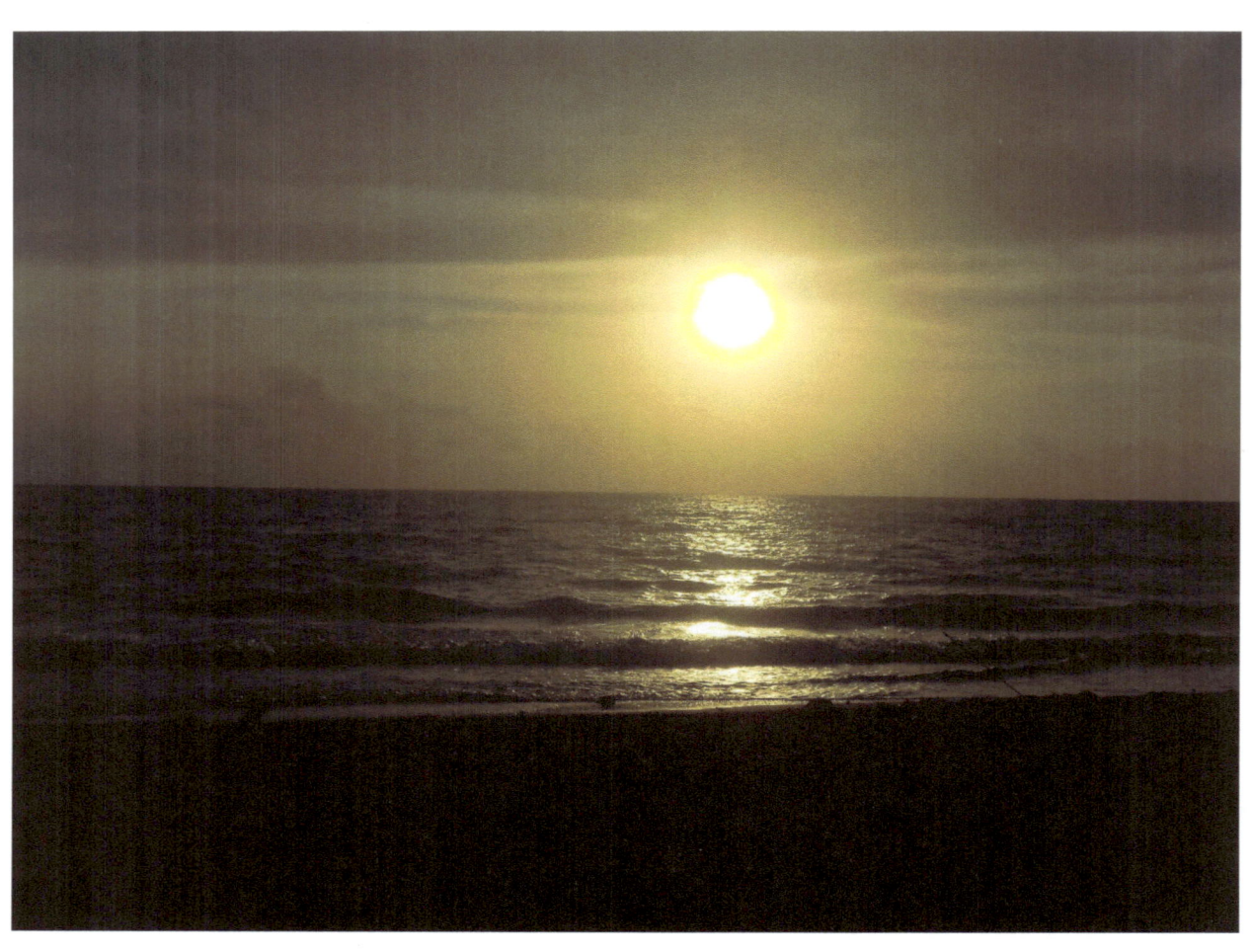

Beginning of the day at Hollywood Broadwalk.

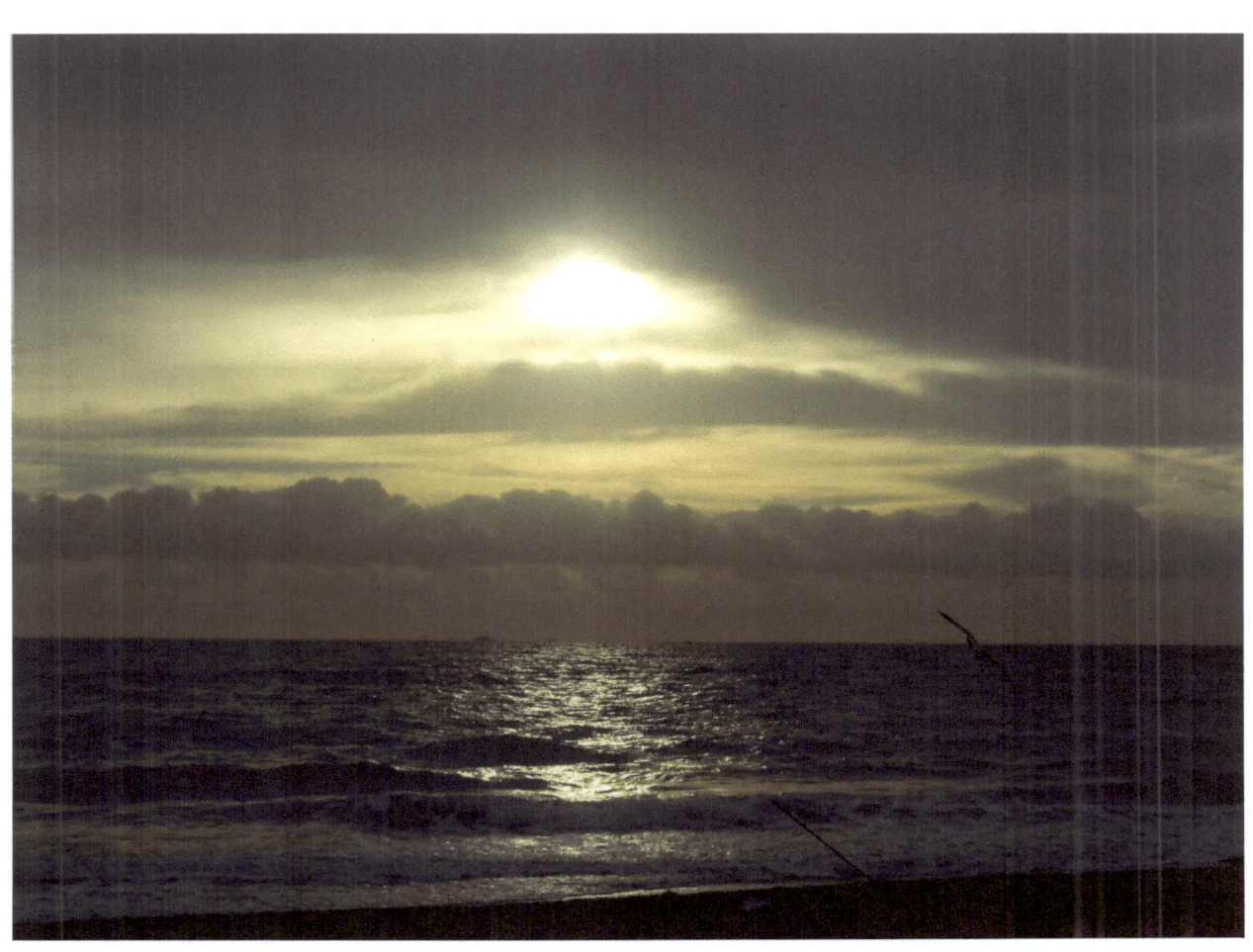

Cloudy and windy morning on the Hollywood beach.

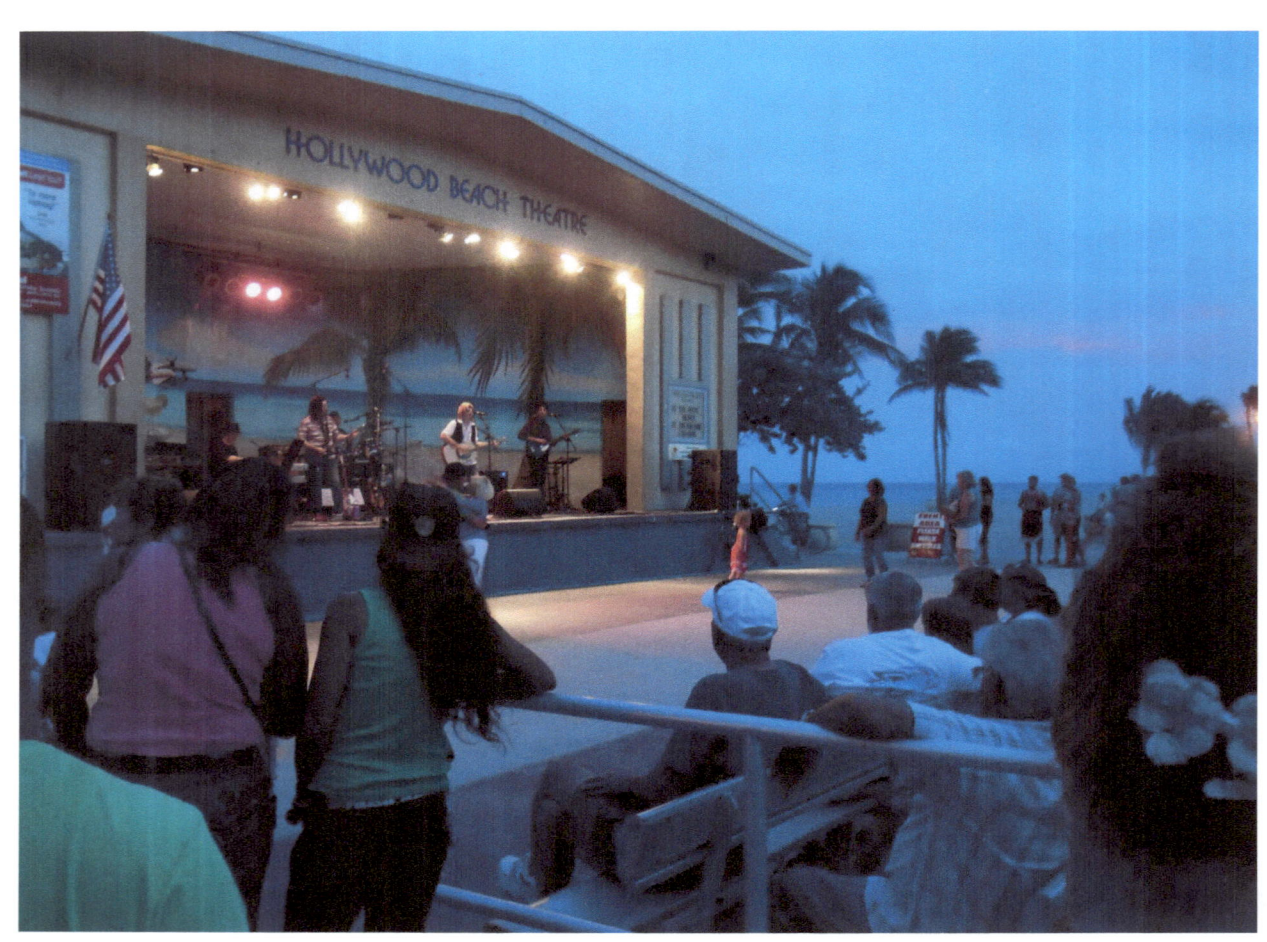

Hollywood Beach Theater.

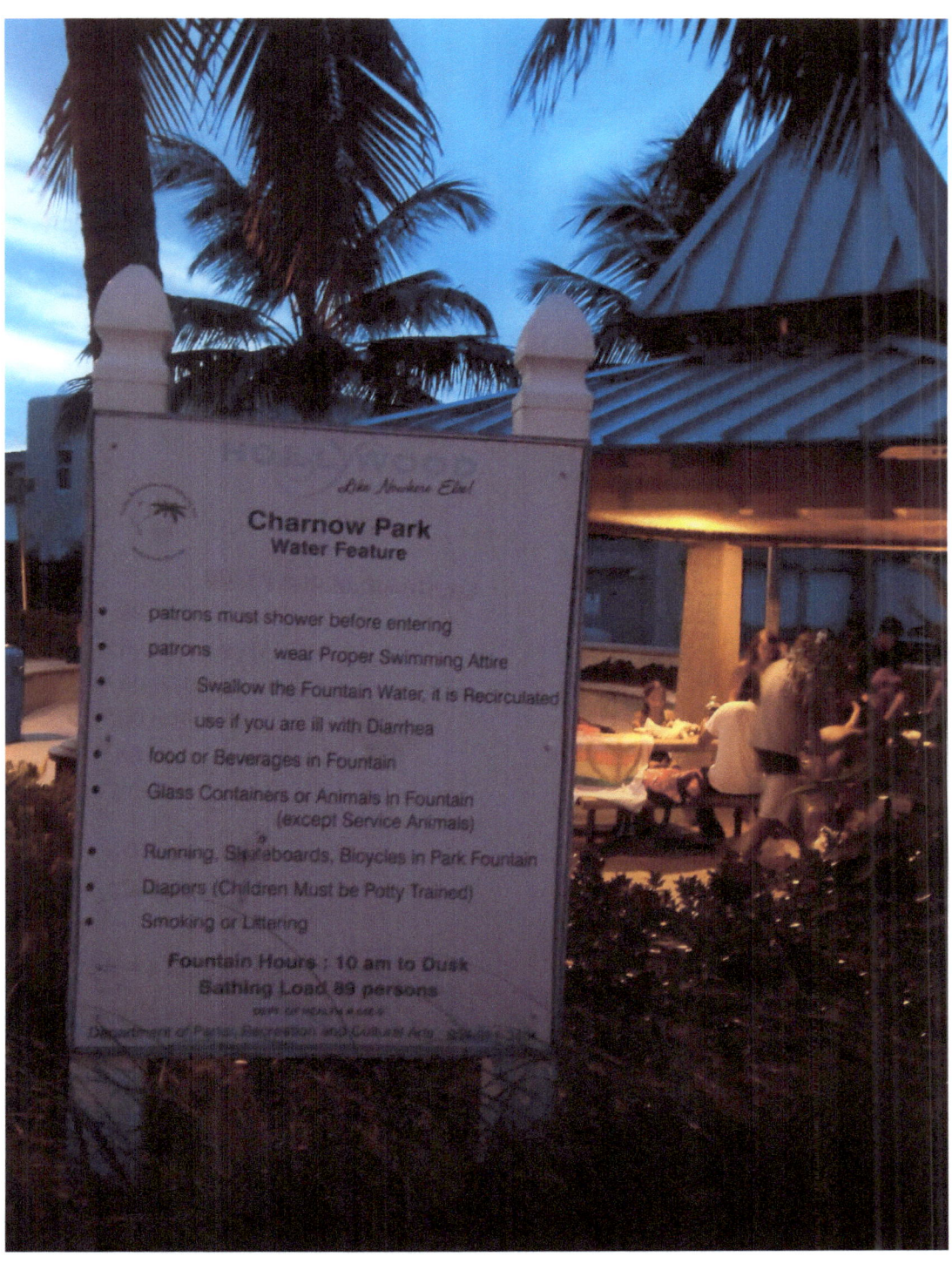

At the Charnow Park. There's nothing wrong with this sign. It is just the photocamera didn't capture the words written in light blue, unintentionally making it look funny.

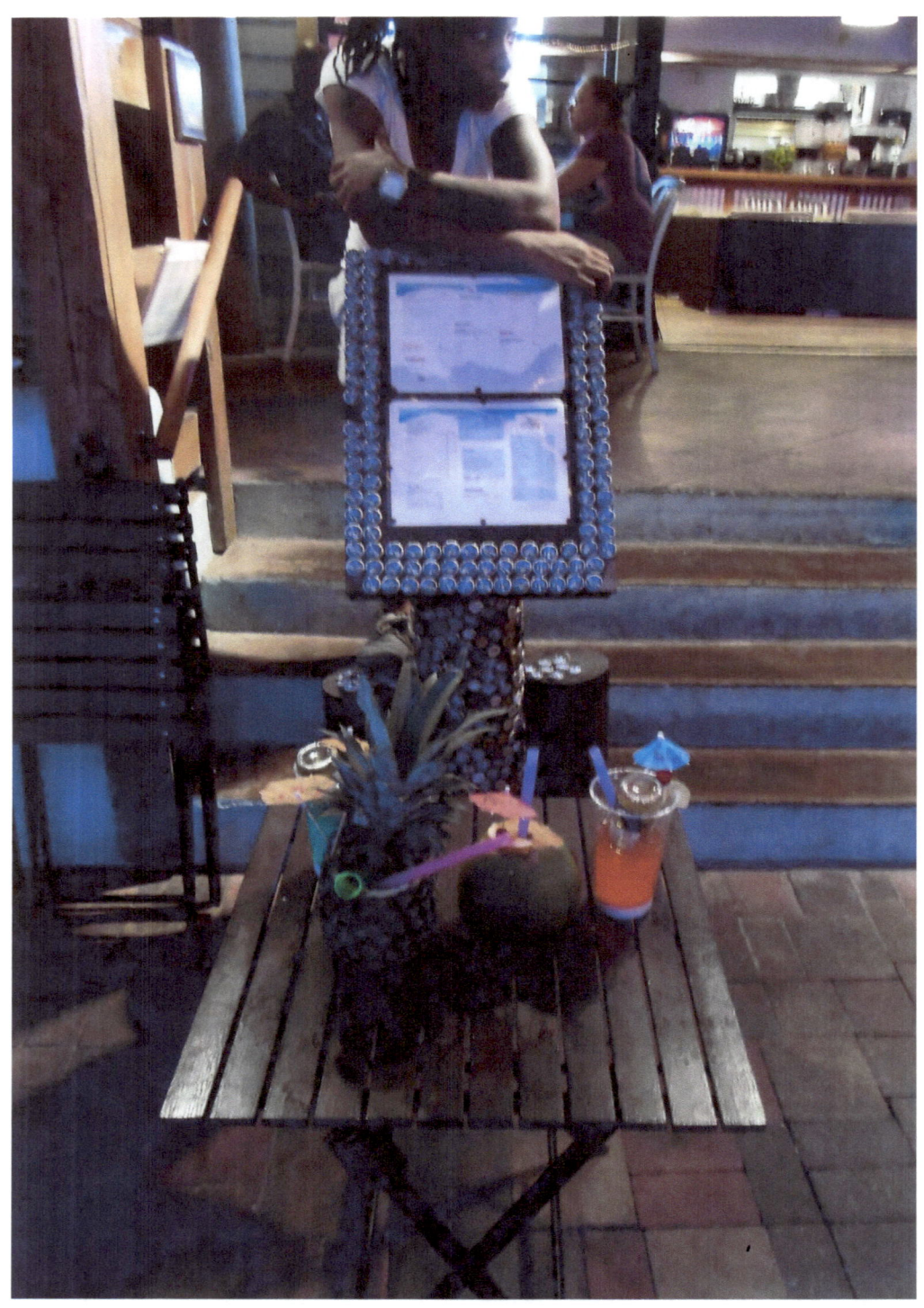

Variety of drinks on Broadwalk.

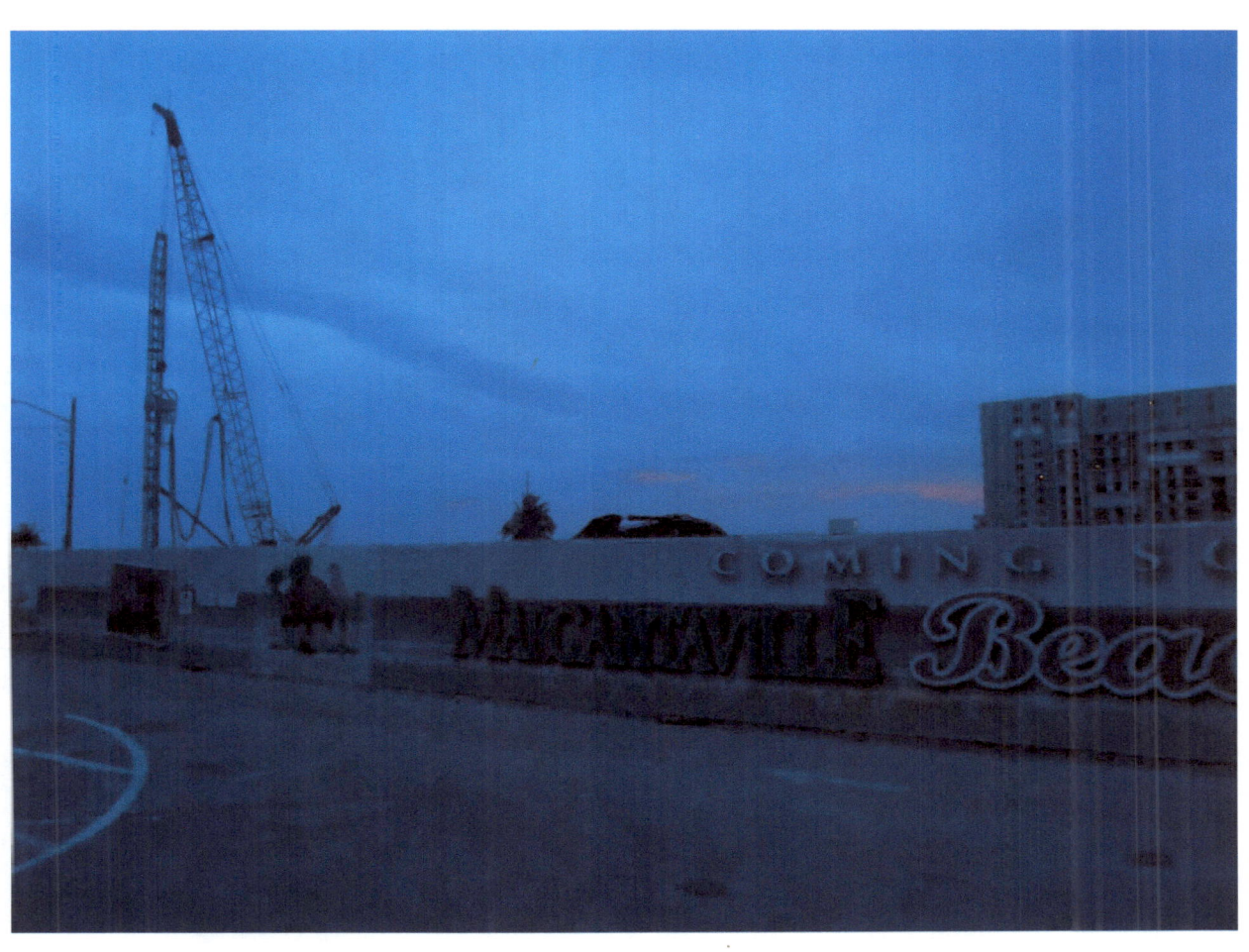

Margarittaville Resort under construction.

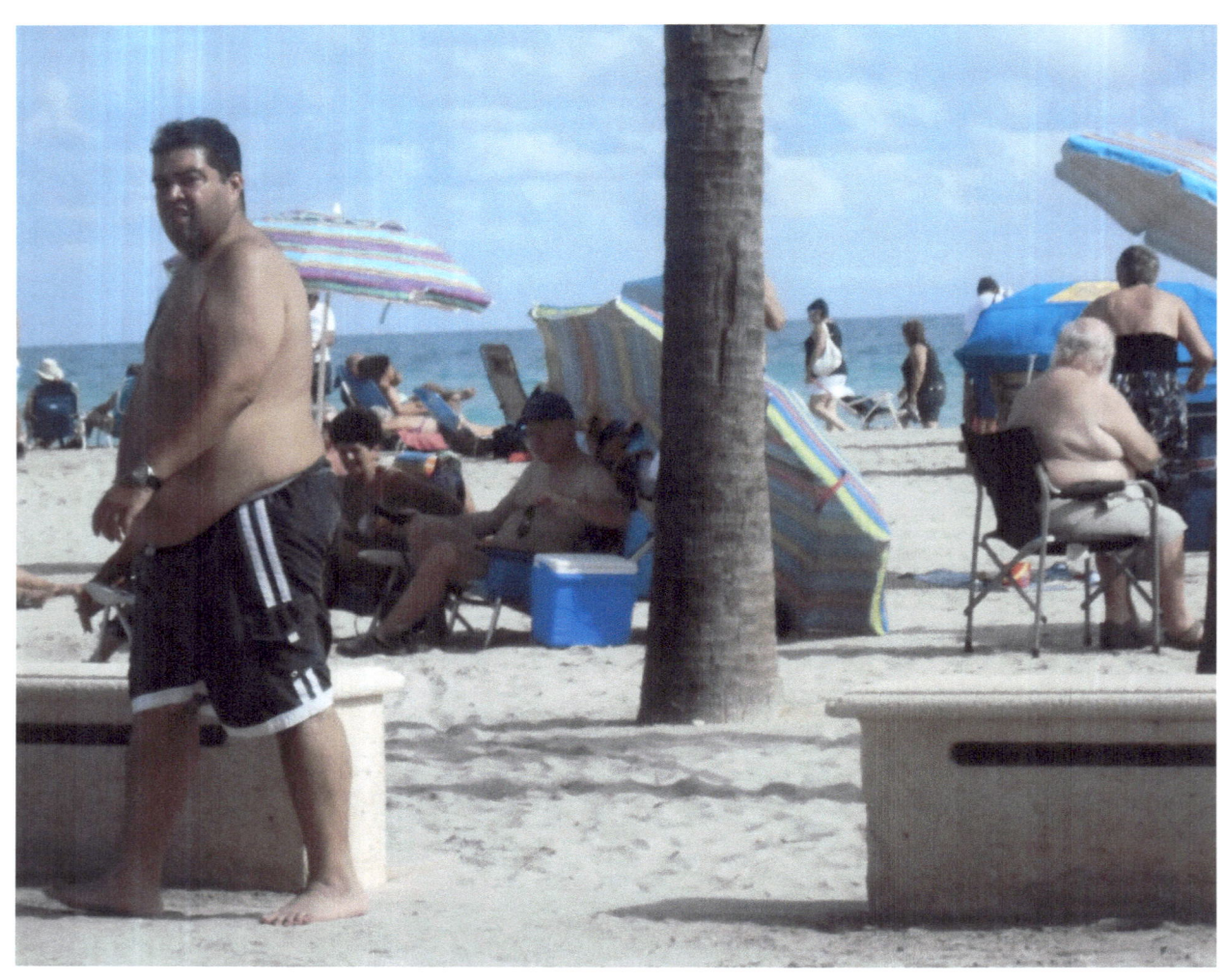

Lazy life.

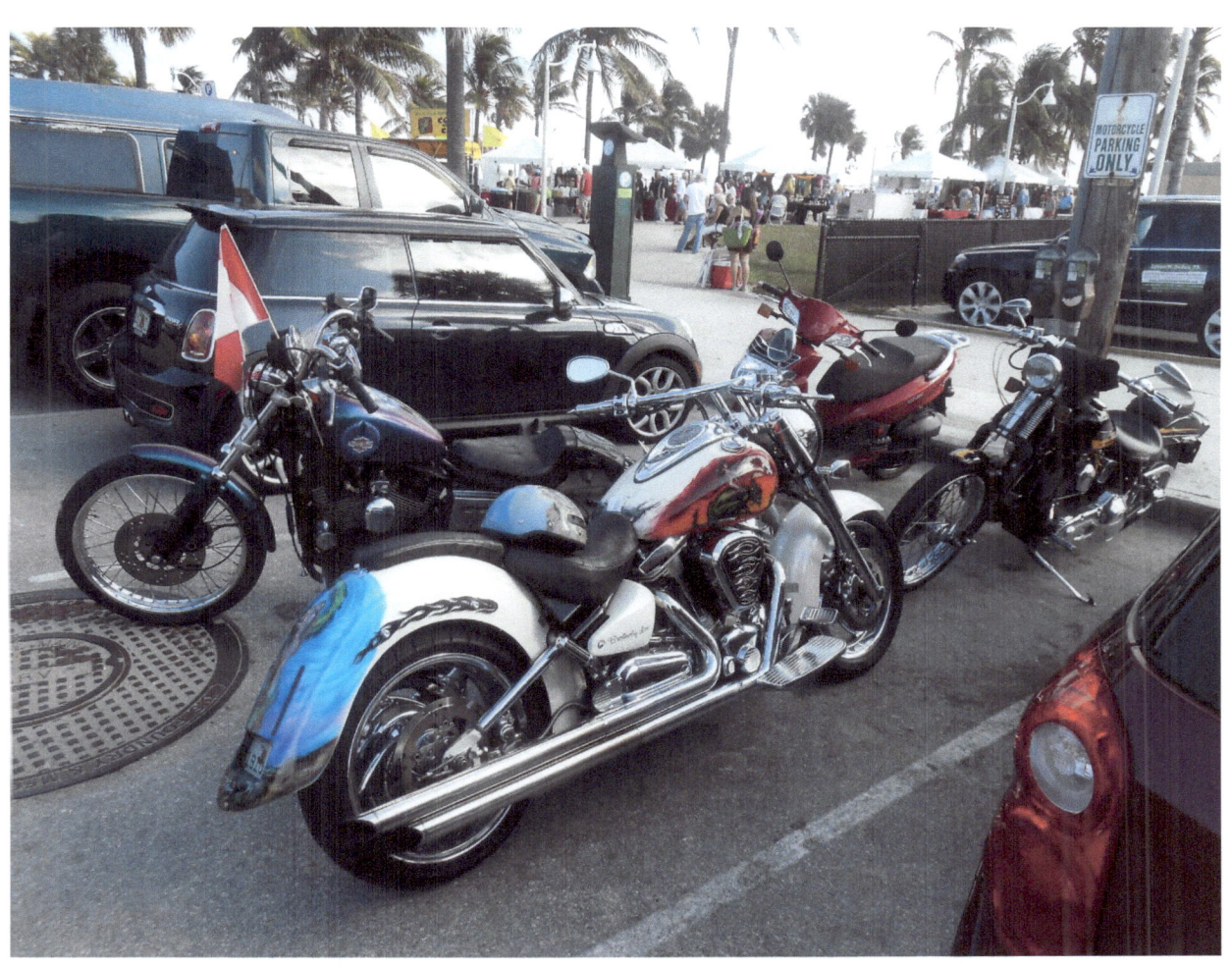

Bikers also have their favorite spot on the Broadwalk, in a bar near Hollywood Beach Theater.

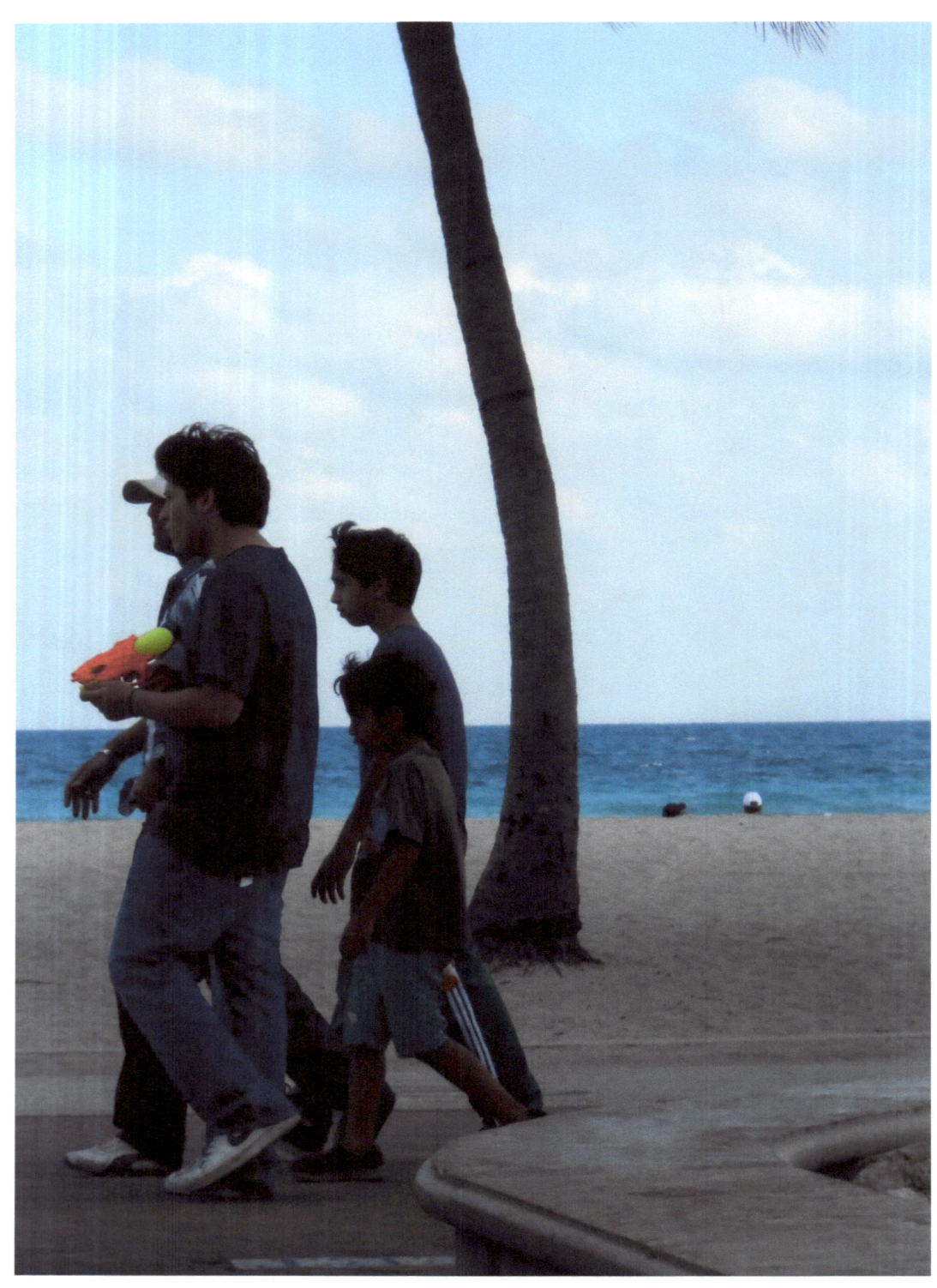

Immigrants in Paradise.

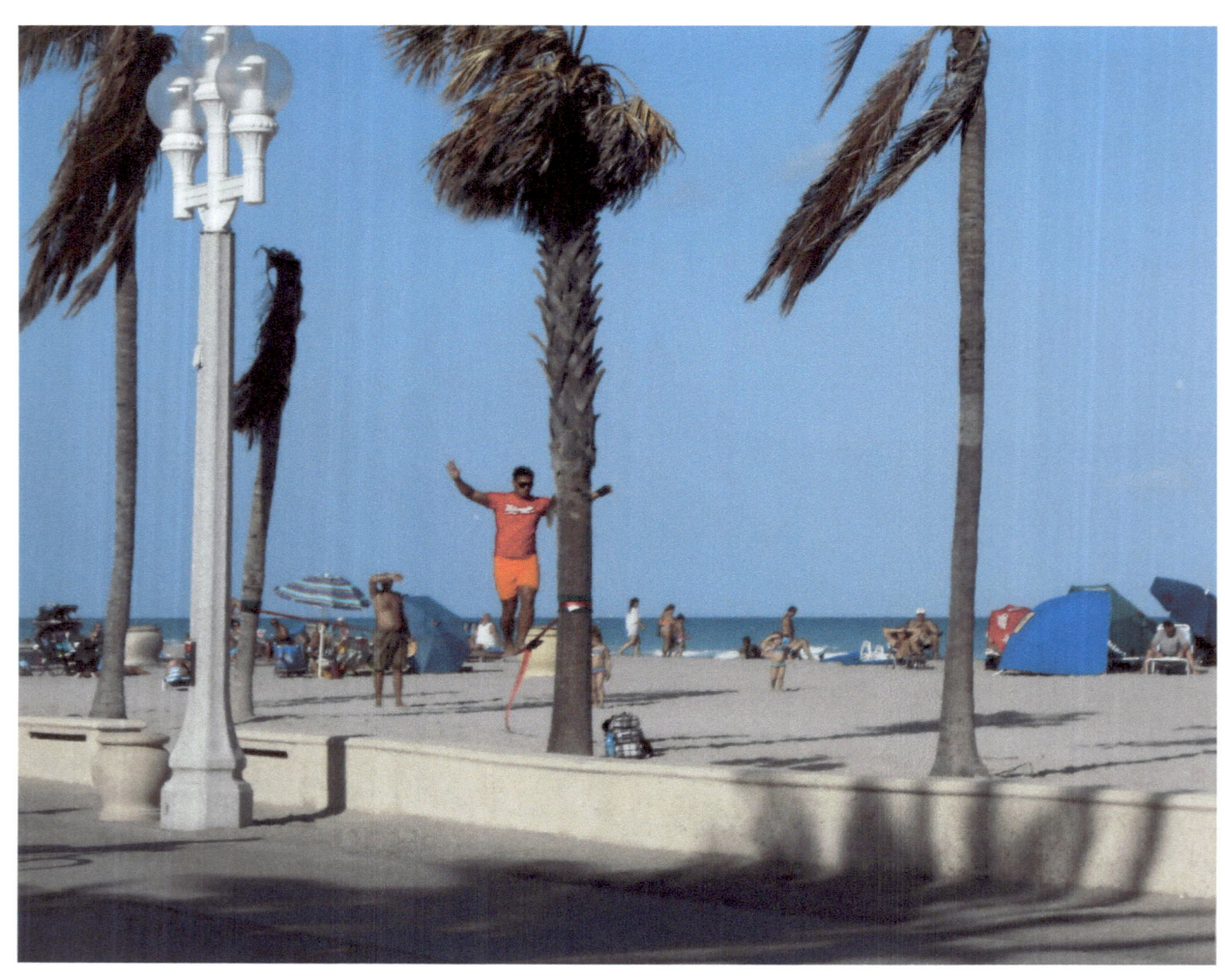

Another way of entertaining self and others.

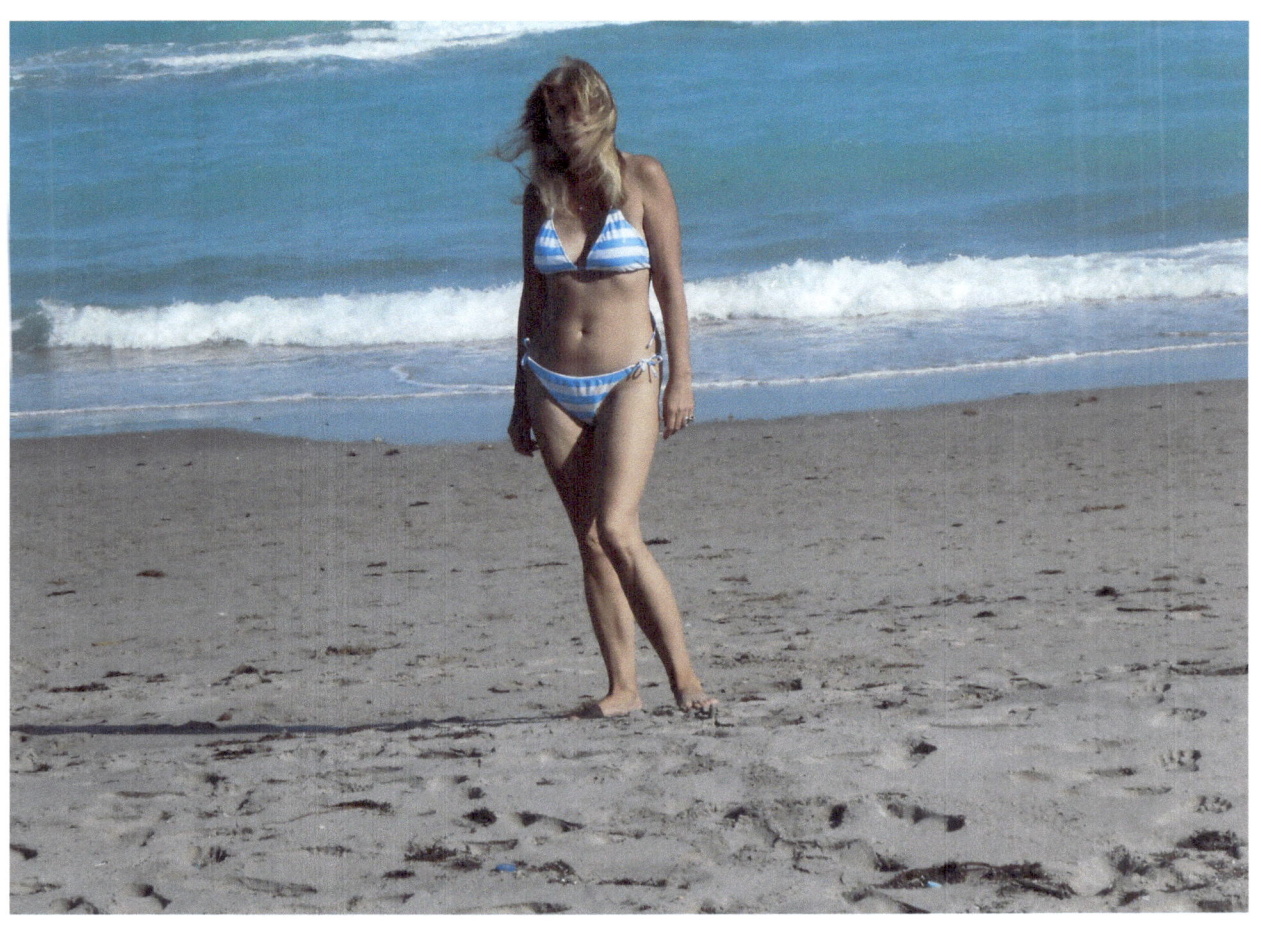

Nadia Russ in Hollywood. This particular photograph has been made by the passing

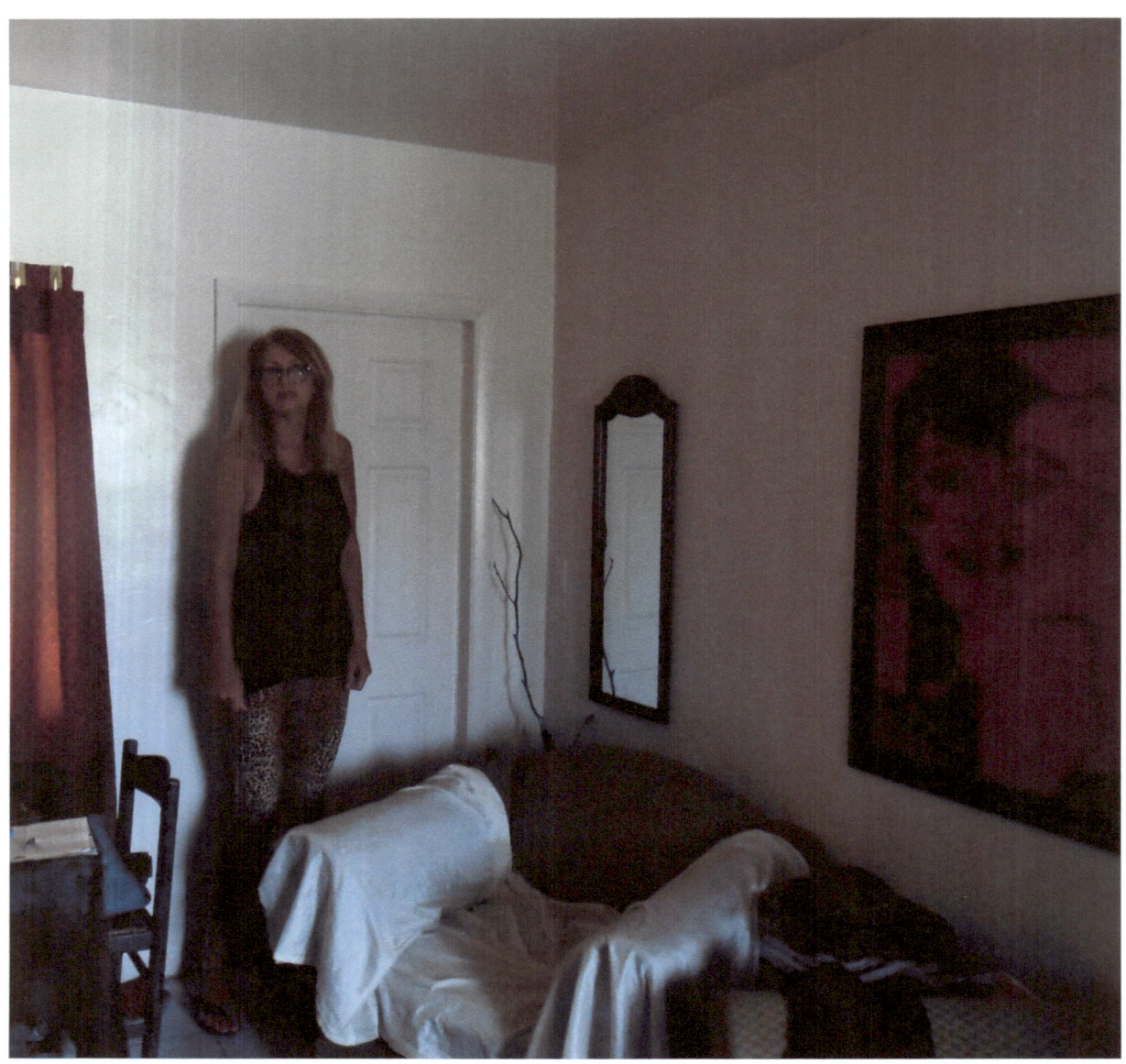

Two minutes walking distance to Hollywood beach's Broadwalk, here, Nadia Russ spent 12 months. It is possible to make more beautiful almost every ugly hotel's room just by adding some style into interior design. However, the life in a small town and a small building, even if it is a paradise area, often brings the feeling of being locked in a box. Then, one breaks the chains and gets the airplane ticket to high energy's City of New York.

Flying from Florida to New York City. Come with Nadia!

About Hollywood, Florida

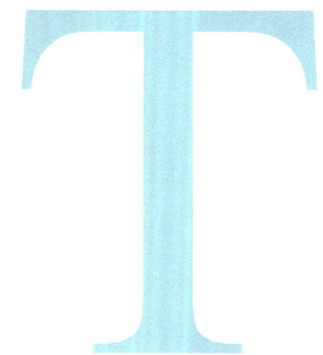he City of Hollywood is located in southeastern Broward County about midway between

Fort Lauderdale and Miami, it is a beachfront community. Today, Hollywood is Broward's third-largest municipality with a population of about 143,000 residents. Hollywood has 7 golf courses, more than 60 parks and 7 miles of beaches.

The average annual high temperature is 83 degrees and low temperature of 68 degrees. Hollywood Beach has several luxury hotels and condominiums such as the Trump Hollywood and Westin Diplomat, the Margaritaville Hollywood Beach Resort is now under construction.

Hollywood is home to 31 charter and public elementary, middle and high schools. It also has more than 20 private schools. Hollywood Hills High School hosts Broward County's first public military academy. The higher learning institutions such as Nova Southeastern University, Barry University, and City College have educational and research facilities in Hollywood.

With more than 10,000 companies in the City, Hollywood has grown into a business hub. The world's second busiest cruise Port Everglades is located in Hollywood; it is home to the largest cruise liners Royal Caribbean's *Allure of the Seas* and *Oasis of the Seas*. Hollywood is home to the Memorial Healthcare System, the nation's fifth-largest healthcare network, and Memorial Regional Hospital. It is home to the largest free-standing children's healthcare facility in Broward County the Joe DiMaggio Children's Hospital.

Historic Downtown Hollywood is highlighted by the Artspark at Young Circle and many bars and restaurants. Downtown Hollywood hosts music festivals, concerts, art exhibitions, and much more.

Fort Lauderdale-Hollywood International Airport offers national and international flights.

Hollywood was founded by Joseph Wesley Young in 1925, who first arrived in South Florida in January 1920. Young's vision included a wide boulevard extending from the ocean to the edge of the Everglades with lakes paralleling each side of the roadway. Since November 28, 1925, the City of Hollywood has transformed to the second-most populated city in Broward County and the ninth largest city in Florida. Young's plan was the incorporation of three large circles of land. These circles became the sites of a ten-acre park - originally named Harding Circle and later renamed Young Circle, the City Hall complex - originally named City Hall Circle and later renamed Watson Circle, and a military academy – Academy Circle, now Presidential Circle. Former resident of California, Joseph Young chose as the name of his "Dream City" the name of the Southern California town Hollywood.

In February 1921, Young purchased the first parcel of land. He paid approximately $175 per acre. By 1925, the Florida real estate market had reached all-time highs. The Hollywood Boulevard Bridge then was built across the Intracoastal Waterway at the cost of $110,000. By January 1926, Hollywood had 9 hotels, 36 apartment buildings, and 252 business buildings either completed or under construction. The city had grown. The construction was rapidly transforming the coastline, it was underway on the Hollywood Beach Broadwalk, a unique 30 feet wide promenade, stretching for a distance of one-and-a-half miles.

September 1926, a hurricane slammed into the South Florida. Hollywood was devastated by the high winds and surging waters. Hurricane ripped electrical wires down, tore roofs, and flattened houses. The growth of Hollywood stopped overnight and Young led in the rebuilding of Hollywood as a head of the Hollywood Relief Committee. However, thousands of Hollywood's residents abandoned their new homes and returned to northern cities. The population of Hollywood declined from 18,000 to approximately 2,500.

Young lived in his "Dream City" up until April 1934, when he died in his Hollywood Boulevard home of heart failure at the age of 51. Hollywood's population had risen to 4,500 in 1935 and to 6,239 in 1940. During the World War II, the military academy site was taken over and converted into the United States Naval Air Gunners' School. The Hollywood Beach Hotel became the United States Naval Indoctrination and Training School. The Hollywood Golf and Country Club became an entertainment and recreation center for U.S. servicemen. In 1945, the city's population continued to grow, reaching over 7,500 and almost doubling by 1950. Hollywood Memorial Hospital was opened in February 1953, providing 100 hospital beds and a major medical facility for southern Broward County. In 1954, Hollywood Boulevard was extended from State Road 7 westward to U.S. 27 along the eastern edge of the Everglades in Broward County. In 1958, Hollywood celebrated the opening of the Diplomat Hotel on Hollywood Beach. It became the temporary residence of many of America's celebrities.

In the 1960s, Hollywood had over 12,000 single family homes, 2,422 hotel units, and thousands of other houses. In 1964, the eighteen-story Home Federal Tower was constructed in downtown Hollywood. It was the county's tallest office apartment building at the time. Hollywood's municipal boundaries continued to grow to the west, north, and south. A population of Hollywood grew to 35,237 in 1960, almost doubling in 1965, and growing to 106,873 by 1970. In 1975, it reached over 121,400. In 1971, Hollywood was the site of the "Pageant of the Unconquered Seminoles", which drew the Native Americans. In 1975, Hollywood adopted the nickname the "Diamond of the Gold Coast."

In recent years, Hollywood has continued to grow, opening new attractions such as the Anne Kolb Nature Center located in Hollywood's West Lake Tract. It is the site of a protected bird rookery and sanctuary and a fish nursery ground. A sea turtle hatchery and preserve has been developed on Hollywood's North Beach. The historic downtown arts district, the Hollywood Art & Culture Center and Harrison Street have become centers of the arts and entertainment of South Florida. More yet to come.

About Photographer

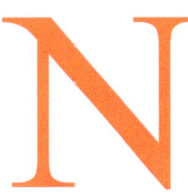adia Russ (aka Nadejda Maloletneva, www.nadiaruss.com) is NeoPopRealism art style creator. Her

work - canvases and ink drawings - was exhibited worldwide; many pieces are in the museums' permanent collections in
Europe and the U.S.. She authored several art-related books.
In 2004, Nadia Russ created NeoPopRealism philosophy for happier life, that works:

1. Be beautiful;
2. Be creative and productive; never stop studying and learning;
3. Be peace-loving, positive-minded;
4. Do not accept communist philosophy;
5. Be free-minded, do the best you can to move the world to peace and harmony;
6. Be family oriented, self-disciplined;
7. Be free spirited. Follow your dreams, if they are not destructive, but constructive;
8. Believe in god. God is one, it is harmony and striving for perfection;
9. Be supportive to those who need you, be generous;
10. Create your life as a great adventurous story.

~~~~~~~~~~~~~~~~~~~ *Notes* ~~~~~~~~~~~~~~~~~~~

Notes

Notes

www.ingramcontent.com/pod-product-compliance
Lightning Source LLC
Chambersburg PA
CBHW050745180526
45159CB00003B/1356